ON
COVE
MOUNTAIN

memoir of a prodigal

IAN DUNCAN

ISBN: 978-1-7342822-6-9

Library of Congress Control Number: 2020909483

First Hammerdown Edition

HAMMERDOWN
Salem, Virginia

His chariots of wrath the deep thunderclouds form,

and dark is his path on the wings of the storm.

−Robert Grant, "O Worship the King"

ON
COVE
MOUNTAIN

For Allison

FOREWORD

Justin Hall

A PECULIAR MAGIC MUST endure in the air of Appalachia, bewitching the hearts of anyone bred here. I know this in myself: an enchantment spread to my bones like an intractable disease, or a spell so powerful it cannot be broken by physical distance, such that when I am a thousand miles away I know some part of myself is left behind, and I am beckoned to return to that country which is my home, nor can I disobey the call, for indeed the mountains own my very soul. It would be impossible to count how many hours I have spent among the trails, to say nothing of all the days my mind has wandered there when, in some distant city, the parabolas of green valleys and the purple contours of mountains remained indelibly fixed in my vision, the way phantom colors linger when you close your eyes to light.

When it was not possible to make a physical return, I would often find myself seeking out hints of Appalachia in the boundaries of my far-flung locale. I spent the better part of six years in Cleveland, a city which, for all its unaccountable riches and treasuries of beauty, is a city nonetheless, caught in the flatlands of Ohio and structured by cement and tediously practical architectures. Entrapped there, the Appalachian spell manifested itself through behaviors that must have resembled, at least to midwestern eyes, something less than sanity.

I never grew accustomed to walking on paved sidewalks, and would unconsciously step off onto grass wherever I found it—the city-curated sod—because the rugged terrain was more familiar to my feet. It was not uncommon that I drew perplexed gazes from passersby strolling along the perfectly functional sidewalks. Or, in the winter onslaughts of lake-effect, in which greater Cleveland was lost under snow, I felt much at home walking across hazardous surfaces of packed snow or ice, in part because I had come prepared with gear otherwise useless in Ohio—a type of crampons strapped to my boots, and my loyal hiking boots themselves—but mostly because, on trails in Appalachia, I have tripped so often and skidded so often and tumbled so often that my feet have developed an intuition for all the nuanced adjustments necessary to maintain balance, in which the practice of stability is a series of unending reflexes.

Or, whenever it rained, I never used an umbrella. On several occasions I even stepped outside during torrential lightning storms, standing in the rain with all but two feet of visibility, surrounding trees leaning madly in gusts of wind and branches blowing to the ground, and all the houses around me shuddering in the thunder. When I went inside, friends looked at me with bewildered expressions and asked, "What were you doing?" And I would shrug and offer some benign dismissal. I could have told them that they ought, sometime, to stand atop a mountain in just such a storm, where every thunderclap is felt in your chest—your very bones vibrating—and every lightning strike so near it seems as though you could reach out your hand and touch electricity. And perhaps I had the sense that, by mere proximity to the elements, I could transport myself back to the place where I had befriended them, or indeed that standing in a Cleveland storm was like meeting a stranger and happily reminiscing about an old mutual friend.

But perhaps this Appalachian magic is rarer still, capturing in its spell only a very few spiritual kin, blessed (or cursed) to wander this wilderness until the last of their days. And for us these mountains become permanent architectures, the way grandparents and parents and siblings and lovers form the very structure of life—and these mountains are more permanent still, such that long after the dead are buried and hearts are trampled underfoot, these will remain unchanged. And however far we venture, however long we linger there, however much we gain or lose, our mountains will await our return and welcome us without a second judgment.

If you, reader, venture from city limits and wander into the tumbledown wilderness of Appalachia to test your strength against the trails you discover there, you will not return without making devastating discoveries about yourself. You will find, perhaps, that you are not easily found, that there is no GPS that can plot your soul on any map, or your life in any direction, that in fact the very predictability you once took to be reality is but an illusion, and in truth you could not tell where you are even if your life depended on it—as indeed it does. You will be like a halftone dot on a topographical map, only visible as an aberration amid all those lines which are heights and depths and lengths and breadths, lines which are like the fine lines in the wrinkles of God's palm. To divine your future from that palm, you must share the vantage of God himself. Otherwise you are lost among them, perpetually wandering, not reading the secrets of providence but discovering them as mysteries.

If, along this journey, you happen to wander into the Catawba Valley and find that your path leads to the summit of Cove Mountain, you may discover on that mountaintop a monument that at last gives some hint of where you are and where you ought to look. The monument there is not made of brick or steel—indeed, it is not a thing made at all, but rock uplifted from the earth in its aboriginal form, knotted and coarse. It does not stand in unnatural straightness and rigidity like man-made spires which point generically upward, indicating nothing but a meaningless ideal. The rock is slanted, its point aimed toward the sky in specific direction, and the whole form canted in the earth in that perfectly relaxed posture of an old man who, at the near-end of his life, sits down to rest. This monument of rock has been christened Dragon's Tooth, which is testament perhaps to the mystery and wonder of this wilderness, as though the first pioneer who walked that summit could only explain what he discovered by reaching into the mythical deeps of his imagination.

If, upon discovering this monument, you have enough courage to climb up and stand atop its narrow peak as the wind blasts you side to side—nothing to keep you from toppling over into the valley below but sure footing—you will be able to look back upon the whole course of your journey, and of journeys that lay beyond it. And if you look long enough, you will not forget the icons of that sight: a diamond-shaped field split by a ribbon of trail, and the ridge that leads to a hump which is a sister-summit to this, and beyond it the two sharpest points of mountains some forty miles away.

Once you descend that monument and follow the trail to the foot of the mountain, two new directions will become suddenly clear to you, as paths diverge in a wood. One path leads back to the place you came from, perhaps to a city of bricks and steel and pavements perfectly flat and everything given to you in an illusion of certainty, such that you will come to believe that you know precisely where you are, simply because the streets have names and the buildings signs and elevators take you upward as far as you can press a button. But the other path rambles off into an unknown thicket, to a place that can only be discovered if you wander along it, not for minutes or days, but for years. And by then you will have found that these trails lead only to junctions, and the junctions to peaks, and the peaks into valleys, and you will realize, not in a moment but in a season of seasons, that where you belong is not in one place, but within that unending journey to seek it out. And you will frequently return to the monument upon the summit—climbing to its very peak and casting your eyes across that immutable valley—to remind yourself, in the grasp of one glance, that the journey is as short as it is sure, and that you may stand only so high as God uplifts you.

PROLOGUE

IT IS NOT UNCOMMON for hikers to become lost on Cove Mountain. The summit is a popular destination for day hikers and bears a moniker nearly as memorable as the three-hundred-and-sixty-degree view from the highest uplifted slab of dolomite: Dragon's Tooth. The trail makes many confusing perambulations and blind turns around rocky outcroppings, and in years past there were not so many signs posted along the way as there are now—an almost comical number if you did not know the mountain's history—signs warning those setting out of the miles of rugged terrain ahead, of the likelihood of needing water, food, and a flashlight if caught unexpectedly on the mountain after dark. These signs are perhaps both a concession to the softness that has befallen the general population as well as an admission, however late, of the mountain's beguiling nature.

I have come across lost hikers myself, nearly at dusk, far from the trail they should have been using to return to their cars. Did they follow the white blazes or the blue? I ask. What blazes? they say. I lead them down the mountain in the failing light, stumbling in the shadows behind me, following the beam of my headlamp through a corridor of trees illuminated like a tunnel, all the way to the parking lot, where we find the rescue squad about to strike out carrying a litter crisscrossed with Velcro straps and duffel bags bulging with first aid equipment, their faces grim and the radios clipped to their belts squawking with admonitions from their supervisors. This is not the first time they have been here. One of the mountain's best known stories is of an amateur rock climber who fell perhaps seventy-five feet from the summit, was recovered alive and carefully portaged down the mountain, over miles of rugged terrain by a team of intrepid rescuers, all the way to an open pasture, only to expire as he was being loaded onto the medevac helicopter.

I have often watched from the summit as hikers far below depart from the trail and unwittingly head toward steep ravines, where so many others have made the same mistake that the strong sign of a trail has been worn there until, at last, it vanishes among the rocks and I see them stop, perplexed. I cup my hands and yell down from the highest pinnacle—this, another disorienting moment: a voice, as it were, from heaven.

"YOU'RE GOING THE WRONG WAY," I shout.

The hikers, dumbfounded, stand frozen for a moment, then look behind them and begin struggling up through the rocks to find the point at which they took their first wrong step.

But I am no infallible guide. I have been lost on Cove Mountain myself. Not merely disoriented, you will understand, but profoundly and entirely lost. I may have hiked that mountain literally hundreds of times; it may have even been true that there were few points on the old dragon and the forest growing along his back that were unfamiliar to me, and that I could have found my way back from any of them—but there was a reason I was there, wandering those trails at all hours, so available to the lost. The reason was that I was the most lost of all.

This is the story of how I was found.

I.

THEIR FACES ARE WHITE and bloated, shining like two competing moons behind the tiny reinforced window. The window is set in a steel door. The door is set in a concrete wall on which panels of dark blue vinyl padding have been attached, much like the wrestling practice rooms at my alma mater. I am the half-naked figure kneeling in the middle of the floor, using the zipper fob on my pants to attempt to unscrew the brass cover from the floor drain. I intend to use the drain cover to smash something, perhaps the window. I explain my intentions, angrily, to the faces. They swear in wonderment.

"This one really is crazy," they say.

I give up with the floor drain and spend the next several minutes running at the steel door, ramming it with my shoulder, screaming—unconvincingly, no doubt—that I am *not* crazy. They unlock the door and burst into the room, hesitating just inside it, bracing themselves for my attack. Behind them, framed by the open door, is the sort of long white hall I will see in my nightmares for the next five years, the sort of hall that would later make it difficult for me to visit doctors' offices and hospitals.

The orderly in front holds out the palms of his hands, covering for the man behind him, who brandishes the syringe. They advance on me as one multi-headed thing clad in white, the looks on their faces those of men forced to confront a wild animal.

I do not remember our fights. How many times, or really any particular one, except for the time I was in a room and moved all the furniture—heavy, institutionally solid beds and dressers—to barricade the door. I remember their sweating, breathless faces when at last, working together, they entered the room, blowing hard and cursing me by the time they got me pinned and I felt the prick of the needle in my ass.

This is the furthest I ever got from Cove Mountain.

Days passed by unaccounted for, staggering those long white halls in a Haldol-induced stupor, the floor and ceiling threatening to exchange places, my eyes drawn up irresistibly toward the harsh fluorescent lighting. Faces, hideous, appeared before me. One, weathered and brutal, framed by strands of long gray hair, made vulgar gestures by his mouth, either requesting or offering a blowjob. Another man sat moaning piteously, the dark purple burns on much of his body oozing fluid. A woman my age showed me the lacerations that lay like a red barcode on the underside of her wrists. She'd made them, she said, with the underwire from her bra, before the orderlies had thought to confiscate it. "I like to cut myself," she confided to me one day, while a group of us took recess in a walled courtyard. She said it as sweetly as a girl might tell you she likes stargazer lilies or the taste of tarragon in a seafood dish.

I became mild and repentant. I asked for a bible, but apparently there were none to be had. I apologized to the orderlies, who crossed their arms and nodded awkwardly, shifting their eyes. I brought Styrofoam cups of water to the burned man when he begged for them, again and again, until the orderlies, seemingly annoyed, told me to stop. My business partner and best friend, Jason Myers, who had turned me into the police, was allowed to come play chess with me using a paper set he had made specifically for that purpose, because they were the only game pieces deemed harmless enough to admit into the ward. He watched me stare at the handmade board, my head floating uselessly, seemingly unable to send the signals necessary for strategy. He had called the police after pushing open the unlocked door of my apartment and seeing an array of kitchen knives stuck in the wall, several more buried in the grain of my oak table, and the words WELCOME DEATH ANGEL scrawled in a huge hand on the wall.

My parents flew in and did everything they could to secure my release short of hiring a team of private mercenaries to break me out, which I know wasn't all that far from my father's train of thought. The panel of psychiatrists authorized to make such decisions were determined not to release me, and to send me, instead, to the state facility, where they kept the really serious cases, and where, had they succeeded, I suppose I might remain to this day.

But one doctor on the panel remained unconvinced. In him, my parents saw our only hope. All this time, my father was working to repair the damage I had done to my apartment, cleaning, spackling holes, gouging out the grout from the shower tiles where I had used a black marker to write out a poem from *The Rubaiyat of Omar Khayyam* across the white tiles. He went to a home-improvement warehouse and bought the necessary tools and supplies: buckets of plaster, gallons of stain-blocker to blot out the writing on the walls, paint rollers and roller covers and drop cloths, and he loaded them into the back of his rental car and drove them to the apartment he had seen for the first time only a week earlier, when he had helped me move in.

I can't imagine how many coats it took. My father had been a professional painter and remodeler most of his career, or the leasing agency might not have accepted his work in lieu of the fine they intended to impose upon me. I can see him there now, rolling out those walls with his teeth gritted and his eyes clenched in pain, and what he must feel as a father in that moment is still—nearly twenty years later at the time of this writing, and after having had three children of my own—utterly incomprehensible.

* * *

THERE ARE CERTAIN SIGNS that a young man is gently going mad. To trace these problems back until they may be laid at the feet of someone—really anyone else—is currently a popular strategy for repairing one's ego, but I have resolved to tell this story from the point at which I was the one solely responsible for it. Otherwise, we might as well begin in a garden, with a tree and a serpent wending through branches laden with that ancient and most appealing of fruits.

I had moved to Texas shortly after my twenty-first birthday to start a landscaping business with my best friend from college. That we were going to get rich mowing lawns and planting flowers was not an incongruous thought to either of us at the time; neither had we any suspicion that the world had far more ways of foiling our plans—and far more determination—than either of us ever had in succeeding.

I hadn't even finished unpacking when I found I couldn't sleep. My situation was tenuous, both financially and emotionally. I had moved to Texas on a shoestring budget and rented an apartment I wasn't sure I could afford. I had very little savings I hadn't already invested in the company, and no car of my own except the company work truck that I had use of after hours. I had never done any of this on my own, and now I was attempting to do it all at once.

We started work the day after we unloaded the moving truck. No matter how hard I labored during the day, hauling bags of mulch, weeding, dragging branches, raking—I still couldn't sleep. I wandered my apartment among the boxes I had yet to unpack, smoking the little cigarillos I was now free to enjoy, now that I was out of my parents' house. I played music too loudly and trailed the smoke from my cigars artfully through the air. One night, I drank a bottle of wine and passed out for several hours.

The sleeplessness continued for an entire week. One night, for reasons I can't remember—perhaps in some subconscious effort to shock by body—I climbed over the locked gate of the apartment complex's swimming pool and jumped in. It was February.

No illegal drugs were involved in my decline. This evil was within me; I had carried it all that way, across state lines, from some familial Appalachian darkness that I had begun to culture, in my own way, in my apartment. Something runs in our family. One of the darker stories passed down from my father's side was of his uncle, dead in his house for several days before they found the body. It appeared that he had killed himself, though his brother never would believe it. My father's mother shot herself once, and several times was committed to an institution. From stories like these, I knew just enough about mental hospitals and psychiatrists to be morbidly afraid of them.

Whatever opportunity my nature previously lacked, I now volunteered. My genetic predispositions and unchecked foolishness now strolled hand in hand. A virgin too long, I had a fantasy of starting a relationship and finally having sex. Like so many in my generation, instead of meeting an actual woman, I settled for the convenience of an image search on the internet, giving my credit card number in exchange for what amounted to a fleeting palpitation of the heart, joining a line of lonely men millions long, contributing to the internet's most profitable business, and surrendering my mind to the vice that would haunt me for the better part of the next decade. You see, long before I seized a marker and wrote WELCOME DEATH ANGEL on the wall, I had invited demons into my soul.

I became increasingly paranoid. I kept the blinds closed and peered through the slats. I began hearing things no one else heard. Voices, always around the corner or on the other side of walls, as though I had begun eavesdropping on a parallel dimension.

On the morning of the ninth day without sleep, I refused to open the door when my business partner came to pick me up, only holding one eye to the peep hole, sure that the police were just out of sight and that my friend was participating in an elaborate ruse. What crime I imagined I was guilty of, I could not begin to tell you. Removing the label from a mattress, maybe. Perhaps the guilt I felt stemmed from my embrace of some form of an anti-life: a mind of endless wakefulness and lust, more akin to a vampire than a human.

That was the last day. It might have been the last day of my life, but for the unlikely contents of the mind which delusion had gripped. In it were thousands of bible verses, memorized as a child in the AWANA clubs, countless sermons, bible stories, and wholesome books. By some terrible extremis, I was about to demonstrate the truth of those proverbs clung to by Christian parents; that, in a most significant way, a child correctly raised cannot depart from his upbringing. I attempted to divorce it, but it would not leave me entirely. This was the beginning of my Christ-haunted years. Had any other paradigm been dominant in my mind but the eschatology of the bible, I have no doubt that I would be dead. If, for instance, violent video games or horror movies or any lesser worldview had formed the ballast of my early mind, that night might have gone very differently.

I have already described, in part, the ways I defaced my apartment, what was, as nearly as I could make it, an orgiastic rite of pagan mania, smoking and masturbating and slinging shaving cream from my fingers at every surface, writing on the walls messages at once obscene and biblical, the ranting of a demon.

By nightfall, by no segue that I can remember, a kind of apostolic simplicity began to appeal to me. I would leave the apartment and I would die. Of that I was as certain as any martyr. Only I would take no belt or extra tunic for my journey. No weapons. I left a Glock nine-millimeter lying unloaded on the table. I carried no money, no wallet, not even my driver's license. I was going to another realm, but I was going there bloodlessly, to be assumed into heaven like Elijah, or to step through a Narnian portal from this world into the next. Nothing artificial could go through. I removed even my contact lenses. I would have no sight but faith. I wore only the simplest of clothes: a button-up shirt, a pair of khaki pants, my Justin ropers, and an oiled cotton raincoat. I took the keys to the company work truck and walked out of the apartment without locking the door or turning to consider the tableau I left behind.

THE POLICE FOUND ME in the middle of the night, wandering the perimeter of a shopping mall. At the last, as though they needed any convincing, I provided a striptease while standing atop a concrete piling. I did this deliberately, to show them that I was not carrying any weapons. I did everything that night for one or another peculiar reason; but I am certain it would not help anyone else understand, even if I was able to fully elucidate the ticker of thoughts running through my head. Suffice it to say I was never unthinking or irrational; the reasons I had for doing things simply had no basis in reality.

I don't know how I drove the truck without my contact lenses—I was, at that point in my life, more than six diopters nearsighted in each eye—but somehow I did. I parked the truck and ran across a busy thoroughfare, horns blaring at me and headlights from nowhere suddenly glaring, all depth perception lost and my astigmatism turning the illumination of that urban landscape into a swirling phantasmagoria of the type that Vincent Van Gogh might have painted from the window of his asylum.

The shopping mall, at that hour, was shuttered and largely abandoned. A man on a bicycle passed me with a curiously cheerful greeting and disappeared into the darkness. I found the mall entrance and picked several half-finished cigarettes from the little forest of nicotine-stained butts jabbed into sand atop a trash can.

Blurry shapes hurried by me.

I asked for a light.

None did.

I crawled into the center of a hillside of bushes that smelled strongly of cedar, and decided that cedar must be the very scent of the afterlife. I lay there on the hard-packed dirt for a while, as uselessly as I had lain in bed every night for the past eight nights, wishing I could sleep, knowing, instinctively, that sleep was the panacea, sleep was the antidote. Once I started shivering uncontrollably I got up and moved on.

It must have been almost a relief for the police to find me, though I don't remember feeling relieved when I was wrestled to the ground naked and pressed, face first, into the coarse texture of the macadam and handcuffed. I realize now what a mercy there was in the swiftness of their violence, compared to the ineptitude of the orderlies' attempts at hand-to-hand combat. I rode to the police station on the plastic-covered backseat, naked, streetlights passing through the car while the police scanner squawked and I rambled to the officers on the other side of the backplate about God knows what.

At the police station, I was returned into my clothes as well as the handcuffs would allow, and after being seated on a folding metal chair in a room lit by bright fluorescent bulbs, I was subjected to a litany of questions, repeated over and over. Whatever charmed peace my delusions had wrought upon me soon turned to outright fear.

I was wheeled, it seemed (the reader will understand that my senses had become increasingly unreliable) through a series of underground tunnels, sitting in a wheelchair or perhaps lying on a gurney, looking up at the joyless gray faces of the officers escorting me.

Do you have a living will? a voice from somewhere asked. I did not know what a living will was, but in my paranoid, sleep-deprived state I rearranged those words into "Do you have a will to live?" the sort of question, perhaps, that an executioner might ask, sarcastically, before raising his axe. I began to be very afraid. And that fear, was, of course, the source of the violence to come.

I watched the police officers check their weapons in something that looked like the drawer of a bank drive-thru, and then we were buzzed into the hospital. Years later, I would discover, by examining copies of the paperwork from that night—paperwork that I went to some lengths to obtain—that I was diagnosed only two hours later. I was not observed for any period of time longer than it took to try to feed me a sandwich and watch me attempt to eat a Styrofoam cup. I was obviously a raging lunatic. A box on a form was filled with conclusive medical jargon, a psychological category so broad as to serve as a landfill for damaged human beings. No relatives or friends had been interviewed. No inquiry had been made into the stressors and acute anxiety of the preceding week.

A surgeon I later lived with explained to me, rather dismissively, that psychiatrists are only doctors who fail to qualify for a surgical residency, and as wildly pejorative as that statement may be, the events of the next ten days would offer little evidence to the contrary.

By the time it was over, I was spending my days in a dull stupor, playing out hands of cards with a group of zombie-like friends. A cheerful nurse tried to get us to sing karaoke. "Love me Tender." Another nurse made us open our mouths and lift our tongues to prove we'd swallowed our meds. I had a pair of contact lenses again, at least, and was able to lay on my bed reading the books my parents brought me, one of which was a paperback copy of Jim Corbett's *Man-Eaters of Kumaon* that remains a favorite to this day.

An attorney came to meet with me. He treated me sympathetically, wisely appealing to my pride, saying that I seemed to be the only sane person in the ward. He swiftly and skillfully divested me of any hope in contesting a judicial declaration of mental incompetency, and then, with the promise that it would get me released more quickly, I signed away the rights and dignity it would take nearly seventeen years to recover.

They let me out. I was released into my parents' custody on the condition that they immediately remove me from the state and begin psychiatric treatment elsewhere. The orderlies led me into a storage room and pulled down a brown paper grocery bag that contained the clothes I'd had with me at the time of my arrest.

My feet were so swollen by then from the drugs and the weight gain and the salty cafeteria food that I could barely force them down into my cowboy boots. I'll never forget walking out of that place and looking up to see the flag of the Lone Star State snapping in the breeze, and all that sky behind it: unbarred, unbroken, and blue.

A MIND CAN BE a frightening thing; an unstable mind one of the most frightening things in all of human experience. It was impressed upon me, by the psychiatrist I began seeing, that whatever I might do with the rest of my life, and wherever I might go, one thing would remain absolute: I must *never*, under any circumstances, discontinue the cocktail of medications I had been prescribed. I could no longer trust myself, though the psychiatrist did not put it that directly, but used a series of facile questions, almost rhetorical, the type of questions that cause your face to burn upon answering.

You don't want an episode like that to happen again, do you?

If that were not frightening enough, I was warned that the next episode—the hypothetical next episode contingent upon my refusal to continue my medication, that is—would almost certainly be *worse*. I must have seemed sufficiently terrified that the doctor, kindly, did not belabor the point. He was, after all, a *Christian* psychiatrist, and this was nearly impossible to forget—not for any mention he ever made of spiritual matters, but for the huge, benign face of the Anglo-Saxon Jesus pinned to the wall behind him, watching me with impassive blue eyes.

"We'll need to monitor your bloodwork periodically," Jesus and the psychiatrist said. Lithium could, of course—though it was nothing to worry about—build to toxic levels in my bloodstream and damage my liver. At the end of every appointment, he led me into a pantry-sized closet and loaded me up with blister pack samples of the medicine that was also, apparently, a poison.

Strangely, he never asked me the first question about my life. *How are you feeling*, was, for his profession, a matter of chemistry. Was I feeling depressed? We could increase the dosage of the antidepressant I took in addition to lithium. Was I feeling sluggish and lethargic? We could try a different antidepressant. Now was I feeling too high to sleep? Another antidepressant. I would notice a pattern, after some years of this, and the pattern was that the answer to my problems was always one or another of the blister packs full of neatly-formed pills, and the most predictable answer was to take more pills—always more, never less.

Those first months home I wore shame like a lead jacket. Jesse Dunker, who had married one of my high school classmates, and who, years later, would become one of my best friends, says he and his wife saw me at some distance in public around this time and that I *ran* to keep from talking to them. I don't remember the incident, but it doesn't surprise me. I wanted nothing so much as to avoid any sort of situation that might obligate me to explain my return from Texas, or why I had gained nearly seventy-five pounds and now looked like a completely different person.

Doctor's visits were particularly uncomfortable for that reason—not just for the long white halls and the "white coat syndrome" nurses said I had when they checked my blood pressure and found it surprisingly high, my pulse racing. The worst of it was the inevitable opening of my folder, the doctor's smile slackening as his eyes passed over various alarming phrases, and then asking, as casually as possible, "So, are you still taking Depakote?"

Questions like those would continue for over a decade.

At the time, it seemed I was living the sort of waking nightmare Dr. Jekyll must have had when he realized he was not only Dr. Jekyll, but also Mr. Hyde. I could only deduce, from the episode I'd had in Texas, that I had two natures, one manic and the other increasingly depressive, though depression had never been a chronic problem, ironically, until I began taking antidepressants. I began to fear that my mind contained a kind of terrorist sleeper cell, and that all it might take to release those terrorists among my synapses was another perfect storm of anxiety and sleeplessness.

But there was the assurance that none of it would happen so long as I continued to take one and a half yellow pills every day—1,350 milligrams of lithium—the perfectly round pills with the convenient indentation in the middle for snapping, suddenly, in two.

✳ ✳ ✳

IF I LEARNED ONE THING from being a person consumed with shame, it is that far too often we grant our respect for other persons in the form of privacy. Visitors and guests in my parents' house seemed all too willing to oblige me in acting as though the Texas episode had never happened. It became the elephant in the room. No one was so rude as to ask me about it, though in hindsight I wish they had. I desperately needed, though I could not have understood it at the time, an intrusion—albeit a gracious one. I needed someone to pry until they located the wound, then apply some salve—a good salve, not poison. I needed someone to speak something more into my life than recommended dosings of the latest popular antidepressant. I needed a Jesus that did more than stare at me over the shoulder of a psychiatrist.

I began my own research into the nature of the disease that had been assigned me in the hospital: Bipolar Disorder. I read and was both fascinated and horrified by Kay Redfield Jamison's *An Unquiet Mind*. My father, who had a degree in psychology, maintained that everything that had happened to me could be explained as an episode of acute stress, and that the huge, frightening labels pasted upon me were not necessarily true. The more I think about my father's defense of my sanity, the more I love him for it. At the time, though, he had more confidence in my mind than I did. The strange symptoms I'd experienced bore an uncanny resemblance to the all-too predictable behavior of someone in a manic swing. I began to examine my past with the same sort of scrutiny a geologist applies to a volcano: early rumblings here and there, behavior that might have only been teenage foolishness, or it could have been something more, the first tremors of an impending eruption.

I continued taking my medication.

My father invited me to work with him in his construction company, and did far more in attempting to repair my self-image than many parents would have. We went to a Ford dealership together and ordered an identical pair of black F-250s. I didn't have sufficient credit, so he made the down payment. The bank issued me a fat little payment booklet. I was doing things that responsible people did, learning how to live, it seemed, by pantomime. My medications seemed to have stabilized; I didn't exactly feel like my old self, but then again, the old me—the energetic, mentally lively me, the wildly creative me—had not been, apparently, an ideal to return to but only a premonition of my terrible potential.

I kept taking my medication. No one even needed to know about it. One and a half pills, morning and evening, and two of the oblong blue ones now to counteract the effect of the round yellow ones. Before my commitment, I had worn a size forty-two sports coat. Now it took a size fifty to cover my shoulders. I was not so much fat as swollen all over. Strangers in public asked me where I played ball. The body simply recognized lithium as a salt, my psychiatrist explained. What lasting effect or permanent damage this might work upon my body was a thing not necessary to consider. The medicine was, after all, saving me from myself, day by day.

Life provided certain compensations. I drove a truck that people admired. I started attending a new church, where I could begin again, where no one knew that I had once looked or acted differently than I did now. Girls from my Sunday school class invented reasons why I needed to drive them places in my big diesel truck. I had a good job; my father and I had begun building a row of patio homes. A future was opening up for me—not exactly an honest one, but a future nonetheless.

☀ *☀* *☀*

I LEFT MY FIRST serious girlfriend in the middle of a ski trip in Utah. Just called a taxi and left in the middle of the night. (Just so you know, that's not a thing that manic depressives do; that's a thing assholes do.) It matters little now, who said what, what betrayals and barbs had been traded back and forth, what had been broken and put together again, poorly, like a child gluing china to cover an accident.

The more significant thing was the pattern that emerged in my relationships, facilitated, in part, by the dullness the medication lent me. You might not have noticed this unless you had known me both before and after—and almost no one in my life did. Whereas I had once been energetic and thoughtful—perhaps *too* thoughtful—I was now listless and calm to the point of being robotic. I went to work. I made my truck payments. I looked online for someone to date. I found someone to date and dated the first girl I hit it off with. Nothing about her really bothered me, at first. Perhaps it was enough that I was dating someone and that she was excited about me. Whatever criteria I once employed—even aesthetic judgments I might have once made—were suppressed. Her faults appeared to me as one might see an object through deep water. She was, thankfully, returning the favor by overlooking my own faults. The danger of this, of course, was that dissatisfaction and irritation gradually built, like floodwater behind a dam, until the things I had been able to ignore assembled themselves against my consciousness with undeniable mass and volume.

Certain things had irritated me, but sex had been frequent enough to mitigate their effect. We talked of getting married, but she wanted to hyphenate our last names rather than taking mine. It seemed it was to be a conjunction rather than a union. Her greatest fault was that she didn't know me; my greatest fault was that I didn't know myself sufficiently to inform her.

I took her to Cove Mountain once. We hiked up to Drag-on's Tooth and kissed for a while, waiting too long and watching the sun sink behind the purple ridges with little thought for the miles awaiting us on our return. It began to grow dark, almost painfully dark. What descends upon that forest every night is not darkness of the type that suburbanites know, a night made intermittent by streetlights and the incandescence of a skyward haze; this is a darkness absolute, as thick and impenetrable as oil.

I led her by the hand, but the mountain, for her, seemed to hold some terrible presence, her eyes drawn irresistibly into the crepuscular depths between the trees, where shadows coalesced into horrible silhouettes.

"*What is that?*" she screamed.

I looked and saw nothing. A stump maybe. I stopped and held her, letting her sob against me.

It grew even darker, not even the deep blue twilight visible now beyond the trees. I led us by the light of the tiny LCD screen on my open phone, an old flip phone that had no built-in flashlight and provided barely enough illumination to see the leaf litter trampled on the trail. I progressed cautiously and found that I could tell when I departed from the trail by the sound it made: the sound of uncompressed leaves crunching underfoot.

We tramped through a muddy spot made perennially wet by a spring that trickles across the trail. My girlfriend cried all the harder now because she feared her white tennis shoes were ruined. I led grimly on, feeling even worse because I had little genuine sympathy for her fear and because I felt it revealed something more significant about her, though for a time my guilt would distract me from those conclusions. The mountain was to me, even in the dark, a thing of beauty. With the disappearance of the sun, we became trespassers in the night made for beasts to roam. Bears clawed and snuffled through rotten logs for grubs. Raccoons sat on their haunches by still pools, caressing the water for crawfish. Deer bounded away from us, snorting, shocked to find a man and a woman in that paradise from which they had been rightfully expelled.

My girlfriend sobbed all the way back to the truck. That night, I learned to think of Cove Mountain as a wild in which the soul of a person could be tested. It was not a test I thought, at the time, to apply to myself. I was a thing, along with the beasts, that seemed to belong in those woods; whatever terrors the gentle night there held, I bore more of them away from the mountain than it retained.

The peculiar thing about my new life—had I the mental clarity to consider it—was that I was still pursuing the same pleasures I had so recklessly entertained those sleepless nights in Texas, only I had learned to go about it in an adult manner. I smoked when my parents weren't around so as to not upset them. I looked at pornography behind closed doors. I successfully traded my virginity for a sexually transmitted disease—albeit a minor one. All in all, I was learning to practice my sins in a functional manner. I was not rushing toward any precipice; I was only taking what C.S. Lewis called "the gentle slope underfoot." I was not headed for any impending breakdown; I was only headed toward hell.

MY STINT IN THE psychiatric ward had only lasted ten days, but the nightmares of it would continue for another five years. Sleep was, for me in those years, a welcome oblivion, the only time I could temporarily set aside the weight of depression like Pilgrim unburdening himself of Sin. Nights the terrors and sweats came I woke feeling cheated. If relief could not be found in sleep, I supposed it could not be found anywhere. I stood for unaccounted periods in the shower, my eyes resting unfocused on the pure white tiles around me, reliving scenes that came to me with the clarity of a vision. When the water ran cold the reverie was broken. Always helpful, my psychiatrist increased the number of oblong blue pills.

I came closer to getting counseling from a doctor at a family practice who had wanted to know the rough outlines of my life. "It sounds to me," he said, "like you have plenty of reasons to be depressed." I remember hanging my head, but I don't remember ever considering that there might be any solution so durable and real as depression itself, no champion that could face that goliath.

One of the best things that happened when I left my girlfriend in Salt Lake City was that I wound up wandering through a Barnes and Noble bookstore and purchasing a leather-bound journal. Nothing ostentatious or fancy, just a small, unruled journal with heavyweight cream pages and a cover that smelled like a saddle shop. I sat down at a small table with a cappuccino in a paper cup, unwound the leather cord from the journal, and began writing.

From the first honest page, I knew that journaling would be the means of something important in my life, though I could hardly have foreseen how much would transpire between the pages of the next nine journals I would fill, or that fifteen years later I would still have more faith in that simple therapy than in all the psychiatrists in the world.

A kind of catharsis seemed to happen on the written page. As I moved the pen across the paper, self-consciously at first, I found myself writing things that surprised—even shocked—me. I was angry, first of all. Angrier than I'd realized. It had been four years and more than a half-million milligrams of lithium since my commitment, but anger exuded from my pen as though, in the process of writing, I had given voice to some suppressed and unavenged aspect of my personality.

I hardly knew at what or perhaps to *whom* that anger should be directed. Certainly not my ex-girlfriend, for her petty slights. I literally wanted nothing from her. Myself, undoubtedly, for my weaknesses and mistakes, but I knew enough about philosophy to know that I was hardly the Unmoved Mover, hardly the master of my fate. That God, as the ultimate source of destiny, was to blame was both the most logical and the least rational answer I could have provided. Certainly he was the one to be reckoned with, but I stopped short of any actual confrontation. God was, in my imagination then, a force of Providence allied with me and closely associated with my own self-preserving narcissism, that sweet sense of self-love that rushes to one's defense after trauma and urges one to preserve one's life and dignity at all costs. God was on my side. He was warm and comforting and much the consistency of a marshmallow. His voice was similar if not identical to the one that alleviates your guilt at eating another donut or drinking another glass of wine because you really have had such an awful time of it. I had little doubt that it was God's will that I should be happy, satisfied, and free; though I assumed, wrongly, that the conditions of those terms would be my own.

I RECENTLY PULLED THAT first journal from the shelf, wiped away the dust of fifteen years, unwound the leather cord, and read it cover to cover one night with a flashlight while my wife slept. The leather cover was stiffer than I remembered and already bore, in the creases of the hide, the faintest traces of white mold of the sort one expects to find on old family bibles. The interior, too, was in many ways not the sort of journal I remembered. I had attempted to format it like a little book, giving it a foreword and titling the entries, beginning many with neatly centered quotations, much like the chapter headings in a work of nonfiction. One of my favorite lines at the time was from La Rochefoucald: "All passions make us commit faults, but love makes us commit the most ridiculous ones."

I had written about the break-up with considerable—perhaps even disturbing—sangfroid, referring to my first serious girlfriend coolly as "the woman I'd been dating," and then launching into a screed about the idolatry of the quest for a so-called soulmate.

I kept turning through the hand-written pages, realizing at once how deeply dishonest I had been, how I had hidden behind platitudes and abstractions. In the next entry, back from Salt Lake City, I had "the painful task" of packing up my girlfriend's things in a box to send to her "as she requested," with no mention of the fact that she had first asked to see me and that I had refused. I had the audacity, after an eight-month relationship, to pontificate on the importance of taking it slow and allowing sufficient time for a person's true character to surface; after all, I wrote, "dating is to marriage what the twenty-five-yard dash is to a marathon."

I took a moment that night, pausing in the halo of light from my headlamp, to consider if journaling had really been a worthwhile endeavor, and if, even then, I should take back my pledge not to burn my journals after every break-up—a fate that had befallen some of my earlier attempts during high school.

I kept turning pages. At best, there were some truly funny episodes I had nearly forgotten: I had accepted the invitation of a seemingly normal girl to attend a Wednesday night "prayer meeting" that quickly worked itself into a Pentecostal frenzy, a kind of collective electrocution in the Spirit that was apparently all the rage at the time. I suffered through it, "not unlike a hapless white settler thrust into the midst of Running Bear's circumcision ceremony."

I dabbled, too, in the shock value of unvarnished cynicism, titling another entry "Thinking Like a Chauvinist Pig," and advocating what I dubbed the "MOTHER-IN-LAW-BASED CHRONOLOGICAL WEIGHT RATIO PREDICTION SURVEY," whereby prospective mates could be "viewed as though through a time, age, and weight amplification module" to predict "exactly what you're going to roll over and see in the morning twenty-five years from now. (Not guaranteed in cases of adoptions and second marriages.)"

The worst was my sophomoric philosophizing about the nature of the triune godhead, and the frequent sermonizing in which I appropriated terms like *grace, hope, faith,* and *love*—blasphemies, all, had you known my secrets. I did admit, after staring at the ocean for a week, that sex had been a mistake. For a fleeting moment, I had the insight that the innocence of my late virginity had less to do with virtue than a simple lack of opportunity. I proffered a weak defense, complaining of our culture's prolonged adolescence and late marriages, how we "tortured ourselves unduly" attempting celibacy long after the ancients would have married us off. It was the sort of self-pity I used at the time to justify pornography.

The only bipolar trait I see in these pages is not my brain chemistry or mood swings, but the division of soul and flesh, of supposed godliness and hidden carnality. I may have confessed, but I did not repent. I continued to profess lofty ideals of romance, marriage, and Divine Providence, but not long before I had driven an hour to rendezvous with my girlfriend in a hotel parking lot, not even granting the marital pretense of a rented room, offering only the ignominy and excitement of the back seat behind windows tinted even darker than the night. How many times had I felt my way, in utter darkness, through the carpeted halls of her parents' house, from the guest bedroom to her door, learning, like a cat burglar, which steps creaked and which did not?

When the girlfriend was gone I returned to online images, a virtual harem to boggle the mind of King Solomon. I established another pattern that would serve me well: confessing—only moments after the act—my crimes against God, thereby clearing my conscience for the interim, however short, between the last opportunity and the next. What I had developed was not a spiritual discipline, but a *method*, a means of preserving, in the face of troubling self-assessment, my alleged virtue. I was no hardened sinner—not yet, anyway. I was, however, a thoroughly self-deceived one.

MY GOOD HUMOR IN that first journal continued as far as my second major breakup of the year—this one much worse, with a ring and a broken engagement and a full set of shocked and crestfallen relatives—and then a kind of dam burst and I dropped all pretense and wrote for ten pages straight about all the things I was angry about, using the word *angry* sixty times before it was exorcised.

I had proposed on a mountaintop in Hawaii overlooking Waimea Bay. The timing could not have been better. The sun was rising over the ocean, the most incredible sunrise I've ever witnessed. It was a sacred moment. I had practically dragged her up the mountain, though. It wasn't anything like Cove Mountain, not wooded, not decorated with random boulders collapsed from ancient pinnacles. It was a grassy, almost treeless mountain with a hard-packed dirt trail that led up to a rolling, narrow ridge more akin to the Scottish Highlands than a tropical island. The only formation at the summit worth mentioning was manmade, an old concrete bunker built in anticipation of a Japanese invasion during World War II. I'd scoped out the location the day before, and had planned to sit on the bunker and watch the sunrise with my soon-to-be fiancé, but much to my irritation when we got there, a lone man already sat atop it, cross-legged, a bible in his lap.

I had to improvise; I dragged her through another little draw and onto another hill and found a spot with a view of the bay that took our breath—or would have, if hers hadn't already been gone. The sunlight shone in the clear and faceted depths of that diamond and it shone in the tears on our faces. She was a colonel's daughter I'd met online. A keeper, too. It had been, by far, the most positive and truly therapeutic relationship I'd ever had. I still didn't know who I was or what I was supposed to be doing with my life, but her family had adopted me with ease and provided a plan I'd actually considered before: joining the military and attending officer's candidacy school.

Her father gave me a crash course in leadership while running in the mornings, and while helping him tile the perimeter of the in-ground pool behind his house, and while teaching me to scuba dive. I disclosed everything about my commitment four years earlier. I told them about the antidepressants and mood stabilizers I took, medications that would, if I intended to continue them, disqualify me from service.

They believed in me. I'd never experienced anything quite like it. They seemed to believe God was capable of *real* things,

real flesh-and-blood miracles in the real world. Not spiritual platitudes. Real victories in the face of fear and doubt.

I began to believe, too. Perhaps it wasn't even so much belief
at first as a broad rift in my fear and shame. I went to see my psychiatrist and stunned him with an announcement. I had decided
to wean myself off my medication so that I could join the military.
I believed with all my heart, I told Jesus and the psychiatrist, that
I was capable of doing this. That God was leading me to do this.
Could he—would he be willing—if I proved stable without medication, to write me a letter to the effect of—I don't know—some sort
of recommendation?

The psychiatrist blinked and his face seemed to harden. He
leaned back and searched the corners of the ceiling as though he
were professionally unable to find verbiage strong enough to express the severity of what he had to say. When he managed to
speak it was to say, in a low, almost quavering voice, that he would
never write such a letter and he would *never* endorse any plan for
me to discontinue or wean myself from the medication. Nor would
he give me any indication how to go about it.

Never? I asked.

Never, he said.

Under no circumstances?

None.

I thanked him as politely as I could manage and left. I was,
after all, still morbidly afraid of psychiatrists, terrified that if I
showed the slightest agitation or perhaps even frustration he
could press a button and call for orderlies to haul me off into long
white hallways. I still had nightmares to that effect.

I left the office carefully, informing the secretary, whose face
suddenly fell, that I would not be needing to schedule another appointment. I left without any blister packs. I never saw that poor
little man again, except once in a restaurant on the other side of
town, and at first I couldn't remember his name. I thought it was
Winter, for some reason, but it wasn't. That was apparently how I
reckoned him, though, in my subconscious: as the personification
of a fruitless season.

I found a plan on the internet for tapering down the medication, one that I hoped wouldn't shock my liver or throw my body into some painful or even dangerous withdrawal. Over the course of the next week, the chemicals left me. I had flu-like symptoms and thought, at one point, that I might shit myself to death. But I lived.

Weight fell from my body. I made the most of my new advantage, running, swimming, and weight training. I lost more than fifty pounds. My friends—the ones who didn't know anything about my past—thought I might have contracted AIDS. I bought and poured over books with titles like *Army Basic Training: Be Smart, Be Ready.* I even underwent laser eye surgery—the painful kind that the military would accept—so I wouldn't have to wear glasses at boot camp.

Most significantly, I didn't have a nervous breakdown. I slept every night. Nights I had trouble going to sleep—usually when anxiety about not being able to sleep was itself the issue—I took a Benadryl to knock myself out. It worked. I was living every day in defiance of the naysayers in my life. I found I was hardier than I'd even imagined. I hiked my old mountains without allowing myself even a sip of water, dumping out my canteens on the summit like a drink offering to some pagan god.

I walked into an Army recruiting station, relishing the great American tradition I was about to join. All the men in my family had done this before me. Civil service and duty were the last things on my mind; this was a rite of passage bar none. This was the proof.

The recruiters, being good recruiters, were openly enthusiastic. Not long after that, two of them drove me to another town in a very unmilitary looking burgundy minivan to take the Armed Services Vocational Aptitude Battery, a test which lasted nearly half the day. I scored so high, when I emerged from the test the recruiters were nearly speechless.

What did it mean? I wanted to know.

It means you can have any MOS you want, they said.

I wanted an 18X contract—military lingo for becoming a Special Forces candidate at Fort Benning—for reasons so stereotypical I need not enumerate them here. Suffice it to say, when I was a little boy playing in the woods with my best friend we called ourselves Green Berets. A man might not join the military to prove himself, but he never outlives the fantasy; he merely finds, in some other conquest, the moral equivalent of war.

The trouble began when the recruiters sent me home with the paperwork for my medical evaluation. It turned out I had enough disqualifications to keep about six men out of the military. The commitment was a bigger problem than I'd realized, and so was the fact that I'd received treatment from a psychiatrist. Also there were the orthopedic surgeries I'd had on my hands for carpal tunnel, which had ended my construction career. The cherry on the cake was that I'd had asthma as a child, and still wheezed from time to time; particularly if I ran in cold weather I sounded like I was dying. That was the one thing I was worried I wouldn't be able to hide.

I went home and filled out the paperwork with complete and total honesty; fine print of a very federal and intimidating nature warned sternly against the alternative. I took it back to the recruiters, who glanced at it, then ushered me into the back room with all the gravitas of frat brothers taking aside a wayward pledge.

Look, they said. We believe in you.

Nodding.

But off the record, they said, if you fill out the paperwork like this we can't even send you up to MEBs.

I nodded. They really did seem to believe in me, that I was strong and determined and capable, that none of the problems I'd had in the past need stop me. All I had to do, they explained—while watching my eyes carefully to make sure they said no more than absolutely necessary—was fill out the paperwork, well, *differently*.

They sent me home with a fresh set of forms, wiped clean of all my trifling imperfections. The future was mine to invent. I sat down to it eagerly, trying this time to ignore the ominous fine print. By the time I was done I had no problems at all. But looking over it again, my heart sank. How could this be the right path forward? A path paved with lies? That couldn't be right.

My fiancé came into the room and paced before me, dismayed by my sudden lack of invincibility. She wanted to be a military wife in the worst way. It was all she had known growing up—the best life she could imagine. She had already picked out a church in Hawaii for the wedding—a church on base you had to be a service member to use.

What was the big moral hang-up? she wanted to know. Lying? We'd done plenty of that ourselves sneaking around those last few months. Why was I suddenly growing a conscience?

I still couldn't do it. Everything about it was wrong, and I knew it. I would only be a trespasser in the military. Whatever strange purpose God had for my life, this couldn't be it. And my fiancé was right, I hadn't even come close to being a man of integrity and that was an even bigger problem, and the peculiar way she'd said it would haunt me for years: You're not *that* good.

Everything fell apart from there.

We had other problems, too; normal relationship problems, except I hadn't been a normal person at the start of our relationship. I'd undergone a radical shift, almost a personality change since I stopped taking Lithium and the antidepressant. I had an edge again. Things that I'd been almost too stoned to notice now bothered me. Something very troubling had happened when I weaned myself off the drugs. I'd woken up one morning with the sensation that someone else had been living my life. A zombie me. And I'd just returned and found quite a few things of which I didn't approve.

I wept longer and harder over that breakup than any I ever had. Like my guts were dissolving. Not just because of the depth of emotions involved, but because of the incredibly penetrating guilt I felt. This time there was no prevaricating. I'd hurt someone I loved. Nearly destroyed her. Not just my fiancé, but an entire family, including a future father-in-law that had given me his blessing and invested a life-changing amount of confidence in me. I wasn't *that* good. I wasn't *good* at all.

* * *

I WENT TO THE MOUNTAIN, and the mountain was there. Unchanged, for all the departures and reversals of my life that year. I hiked along the trail, the sun shining through a firmament of tiny new leaves. Streams ran deep and cold, snowmelt still seeping through the ground, making its way down through unseen channels in the heart of the mountain, emerging again in stone-lined pools where wrens and chickadees paused to dash their wings, shaking themselves dry. Fiddleheads struggled up through the leaf litter, pushing aside the desiccated remains of last year's ferns.

I followed the blazes, climbing over rocky cataracts, choosing my footing along narrow ledges, my heart pounding in my ears by the time I gained the ridgeline, my head crowned with sweat and my blood somehow purged in the exertion. A signpost is planted there, seemingly at the top of the world, and nearly at all times there is the high sound the wind makes blowing through the pines. Sometimes I would close my eyes to listen to it.

A short side trail leads perhaps five hundred feet to a sandy arena where the Dragon's Tooth formation juts from the ground in perpetual upheaval, what is, you realize, when you have spent some time there, an angle shared by the entire uplifted mountain; not quite vertical, leaning somewhat like an ancient ruin, and the rocks exactly the color of a weatherworn castle. The sand under your feet as you approach the rocks has been formed from tiny grains eroded, one by one, from the stones over millennia, the effects of those epochs great enough to be seen but far too slow and patient to be observed. Every handful of that sand represents, I suppose, a lifetime.

I climbed up onto the Dragon's back, wedging myself between two standing towers of stone and getting a boot planted against a hard ridge on one side before I grasped a handhold on the other side and pulled myself up, a few more sand grains turning loose under my fingers.

I stood in the narrow saddle of the rock, the ledge on one side falling away perhaps thirty feet to the sandy arena, and on the other, perhaps a seventy-five-foot sheer drop into the forest that sweeps down the mountain. It's the kind of place that makes those afraid of heights suddenly bend their knees and look for a seat. I paused there to look down into the Catawba valley, only the wooded ridges of the surrounding hills highlighted in a verdant pastel, as though an artist's brush had skipped across them, leaving the valleys untouched.

Everything was nascent in that spring. I felt a man reborn.

I scrambled up the last twenty feet of the rocky escarpment, to the highest pinnacle, a little seat formed there perfectly in the stone. I took my pack off and arranged myself comfortably, swinging my legs over the edge and dangling my boots in the clear air over the valley. Far below, a brief stretch of State Road 311 was visible, that portion of the road from which, if you gaze at this ridgeline at the right time of day, you might just make out the gap between these uplifted stones, the sharpest and most dramatic of which could be imagined an incisor in the mouth of some supine and fearsome beast.

I opened my pack and pulled out what was only my second leather bound journal, its pages still blank. I began the first entry in black ink, titling it "Dragon's Tooth."

"I want to know," I wrote, "the mind of this God, who would create such a wildly tactile, gritty, vivid, and uncontrollable place, and yet govern it with such peace and tranquility."

This was the place to which I would return, again and again, hundreds of times over the next fifteen years, under sun and cloud, rain and snow, wind and fog, hopefulness and depression, in aching cold and baking heat, to gaze at rainbows and circling buzzards, to stare beyond those receding blue ridgelines into the unknown itself, to think, to wonder, to speak— sometimes bitterly—to God, to watch clouds pass soundlessly by, to lay draped over the uppermost rock, shirtless and bootless, the voices of hikers below wafting up, saying I was crazy and speculating whether I was even awake.

This was my mountain. If you were to show me a picture of myself there I could tell you, based on my position on the rock, what season of life I was in. I began as a teenager down in the sandy arena, watching—partly with envy and partly with horror—my friends festooning the highest rock, arms and limbs dangling, but no courage of my own to join them. When I first began to go there alone, I found a spot, further down the dragon's back, close to the point where the canopy of the trees reached the rocks, where the semblance of a stone seat afforded a view of the valley, the approach to it nearly hidden by an old rhododendron growing stubbornly from a void between the rocks. I have stepped that way since, only to find that a pine I once looked over has grown so much that there is no longer any view. After that, I was content to climb as far as the high saddle, but not so reckless as to venture up that final ascending knife's edge, where only a small slip to the left or right would almost certainly be my last. Beginning to climb there, up to the highest point, onto the tip of the dragon's tooth, was, in some small but significant manner, the first step I took toward adulthood. And all that time the mountain, but for its slow and granular attrition, never changed.

A SERIES OF ORACLES appeared before me, though in my youthfulness I hardly recognized them as such or reckoned their soothsaying as more than an omen. Only a year before, a doctor in a white coat had stood before me and told me I needed to end my construction career due to the nerve damage in my hands.

Two surgeries later, I was convinced. My father took me to the donut shop, bought me a coffee and a pastry and sadly announced that he had no more work for me to do. Lending for new projects had been restricted considerably. In our town—or at least for our family—the recession had already begun. A tersely worded, tri-folded letter arrived from my real-estate broker, advising me of the obvious fact that I no longer had any interest in pursuing my short-lived career as a Realtor. There were no houses to build; no houses to sell. I sold my truck and bought the old high-mileage jeep that would carry me through the adventures of the next ten years.

Perhaps because I looked like a preacher when I wore a suit and tie, or because I sounded like a preacher giving the eulogy at my grandmother's funeral, or perhaps only because I could write, people started suggesting I go to seminary. It made just enough sense for me to consider it. I thought of my life at that time by the vague but popular cliché of a long hallway lined with doors in which God was always closing some and opening others in a game of Providential hide-and-seek.

My father offered to pay my way to attend the same seminary he had graduated from in Texas. Looking back, I realize I did plenty to contribute to the guilt he must have felt. What was I supposed to do with my life now? I had asked, as his construction business dwindled. I had been promised various things, my father's most earnest intentions that ultimately fell outside his providence. He had expected the construction business to go very differently; I had gotten carpal tunnel working for him and he felt responsible to help me find another path forward in life.

The simple truth was that my parents loved me. They never seemed to think of me as a boomerang, or as a rocket idling on the launch pad, billowing white smoke but never quite lifting off, always some technical glitch, always some component missing, always some engineer looking at a disconnected hose and scratching his head. They were, nearly to a fault, compassionate; and they took upon themselves a kind of blame for my failures in a way I would not understand until I had my own children. I could not then imagine what it would mean to send a part of myself out into the world, to hoist the dove into the air and listen to the flutter of wings as it departed, only to find it returned some days later, scratching at the window, and to deem, by the olive branch in its beak, that the world, though ruined, yet remained.

I made an inquiry and found, incredibly, that there were two weeks remaining to apply for the fall term at seminary. Everything after that seemed to happen with great haste. My pastor, who had also attended that seminary, agreed to write me a letter of recommendation. He laid his hand on my shoulder and proceeded to offer up what sounded to me at the time like a very strange prayer; not the invocation I had expected, as though the hands of old Jacob insisted on crossing, laying upon some other head the firstborn's blessing. O God, he began, I pray that you would bring hardship after hardship upon this young man. I lifted my head and looked at him, as though shocked by an irreverent joke. The oracle's eyes were squinted into tight crow's feet, seeing some vision I had not imagined or remembering some way, narrow and winding, that I had never aspired to tread. Years later, broiling in cynicism, I would say the old man had intended that God fashion me into a saint, but had, by that strange imprecation, inadvertently doomed me to become a writer.

My grandfather, perhaps the last and least likely of the oracles that made pronouncements concerning me that summer, who routinely saw elephants in the yard and had recently taken a good-natured swing at his caretaker as though to see if he could still land a punch, regarded me with stunningly clear blue eyes from his wheelchair and listened to my mother explain that I was moving to Texas to go to graduate school. He smiled. That'll stretch him, he said.

IN THE CITY, I unconsciously enacted parodies of climbing Cove Mountain. I exercised at odd hours in the common room crammed with the apartment complex's random assortment of treadmills, rowers, and cable machines, ignoring, as best I could, the profane broadcast of the television mounted in the upper corner. Sufficiently taxed, I would run the concrete stairs of the parking garage—sometimes startling unsuspecting pedestrians or seeing other students I knew—running those three flights again and again until I raised the uppermost landing, by some instinct in my mind, to the elevation necessary for a summit experience.

I wandered the uppermost deck, breathing heavily. It was a concrete waste sparsely populated by cars. A low parapet wall was capped by a loose-fitting layer of sheet metal, missing screws at places and moving under my hands when I leaned against it. Beneath me, cars ascending through the levels of the garage sent tremors through the entire structure, faintly pulsing, echoing, and cavernous. The only mountains in my view were vast and sheer ranges of glass and steel, single windows illuminated here and there on random stories, the long perpendicular green stripes of the Big Pickle, the glowing red letters of the Maker's Mark building, a myriad blinking lights, helicopters, streetlights, antennas, ambulances, airplanes circling, an unfocused swirl if you squinted your eyes or held up your phone and resolutely took a picture of inadequate exposure.

My parents cosigned the lease and set me up in a single bedroom loft, what was to me both a beautiful and terrifying space of freedom, silence, and unblemished white walls. Here, I would have a new beginning, another chance to prove what sort of man I was behind closed doors and if I could live with my own thoughts; whether or not, at last, my mind was a thing that could be trusted.

I began to value peace, to savor silence. I'd brought an old picture tube television with me, almost as an obligatory appliance, and it posed a small but significant question about my new life: was I the sort of person that would, for instance, make a habit of watching the local news or catching the late shows before turning in?

After a while I began to resent the unpeaceful squawking it made—even its hulking and monochromatic presence while silent—its dark, curving glass ominous as a palantir. I carried it down and left it sitting on the concrete beside the dumpster with a handwritten note that said FREE TO A GOOD HOME.

I took down books from my shelves and read them without interruption, sometimes in one sitting. Those hours the sun came slanting in, and in every season that did not leave me shivering, I would set up a folding chair on my apartment's tiny balcony, take my shirt off, and bask in the Texas sun. Late at night, I lay on the couch with a CD player whirring on my chest, playing Edward Higginbottom's arrangement of Agnus Dei through my earbuds, particularly Mendelsohn's "Hear My Prayer," watching candlelight transform the high plaster ceilings into a space not unlike a cathedral, and whispering things to God as though by some faint and removed order of priesthood—Melchizedek's perhaps—I had the right to converse with him.

I went to class, of course. I ironed my clothes and drove to campus and attended chapel and visited the bookstore and made conversation and walked about. I studied Greek and hermeneutics. I learned to take pride in acing theological exams. I read the required books and wrote the required papers, but it became apparent, though I was not yet able to admit it, that my classes and coursework were the least significant aspect of my new life.

A nearly unconscious agenda ran parallel to my studies. I was, for some reason impossible to comprehend, a writer. In college I had kept poetry as a sort of mistress, never once considering that we might be lawfully wed, that I might have given up my pride, quit philosophy, and taken up a major in English. Instead, I smuggled reference volumes of poetry from the stacks and pored over them in my dorm, mistakenly believing, as every true thief must, that love and ownership attend each other by rights.

By the time I entered seminary, I had written a fair number of poems and some longer essays, but never an entire manuscript. That I wanted to do something with writing was nearly as awkward for me to express as how, exactly, I thought I might go about it. A friend who seemed to understand me better than I did myself suggested I join a writer's group. She happened to know of one, and made the necessary introductions.

Few things could have been so beneficial to this unmoored soul as to be thrust into a circle of like, but unknown, minds.

I joined them one Saturday morning at a restaurant in Lower Greenville. It was the versatile and enterprising sort of establishment that declared itself a bar by night and repented as a coffee shop every morning. It was not a particularly appetizing venue—not after Friday night had left the tables tacky and redolent of spilled beer and the staff moved about stiffly, and unwelcome sunlight revealed holes in the walls and hastily applied spackle, like pits in the face of an old alcoholic.

The coffee, though, was redeeming. I took stock of the group: five of us comfortably occupying a corner booth with ripped vinyl seats. We were all seminary students, though we would seldom speak of it, and we were all writers. There the similarities largely ended. Shannon, blonde and pretty but unselfconscious, was writing a children's fantasy "with a British influence." She worked in the pastoral ministries department at the seminary and would later be the one to tell me that I had been placed on an administrative watch list for a piece of edgy fiction I had turned in for a class in Trinitarianism. Jenny was sanguine and a natural encourager, and the only one of us already married. She would be one of the first to read my next four books. Jill was quick to laugh and came by her Texas accent honestly. She would always say my writing "rocked her face off" and would be the first among us to earn an MFA in Creative Writing and a doctorate in English. I would later write and perform a poem for her wedding. Joel, from Alaska, and nicknamed "The Salmon King," was dark haired and keen—something of a fox in the henhouse, I figured. He sat with his sweatshirt hood pulled up as one might in a televised game of professional poker. Nearly ten years later, he would be the best man in my wedding.

My life might have still been incomplete in many ways, but as of that moment I had the three most important things any writer could ask for: time to write, a place to write, and an audience waiting to read anything I produced. Other members came and went over the years (one never returned after we snickered over melodramatic dialogue in the Western he was writing) but this was the core; this was the group that would eagerly await installments of my first novel, that would meet faithfully for the next three years, and even after we scattered across the nation, would trade manuscripts by email and drop in on each other during cross-country trips.

Only earlier that year, I had become a fiction writer, and it had happened much the same way you might contract a strange fever. I was in the O'Hare airport waiting out a layover on my way back to Dallas after visiting Virginia, sitting in one of those blue faux-leather seats half the world is familiar with. I sat and watched a never-ending throng of humanity pass by, people of every imaginable description, and descriptions that began to suggest themselves to me in actual sentences, and sentences which began to create fascinating back-stories. The airport became a depot of characters. It was as though two wires, never before connected, were crossed in my mind, and the very engine of fiction thereby hotwired.

I got into Dallas late that night. The next morning, I awoke, looked into a bare refrigerator, and walked down into Deep Ellum for breakfast at Café Brazil, occupying a little table by the big plate glass window that looked out onto Elm Street.

Something happened while I was sipping flavored coffee and waiting for my order of huevos rancheros. Whatever had clicked for me in the O'Hare airport had followed me home. A scene began to play out before my mind, a drama for which the gritty urbanity of Deep Ellum was altogether perfect. Two men sat along the windows, facing each other several tables apart. Each recognized the other, though they were not friends. Tension mounted as familiarity hardened into certainty, every motion at their respective tables—tearing sugar packets, stirring coffee—now imbued with the character of an unblinking standoff. The waitress sensed it and hurried back to the kitchen, watching nervously from the short-order window. When the pistols came out, a fusillade of bullets nearly destroyed the café.

I began writing at my table, forgetting to finish my breakfast. Shell casings littered the floor, the plate glass window beside me shattered. I filled a legal pad, and then another. It was the beginning of my first novel, the inciting incident, transcribed in a white heat, the creative fervor bearing, perhaps, real similarities to a manic episode, though without any of the delusions, dysfunction, or sleeplessness. My only break with reality was to enter a fictional world; my only hallucination was to see, with my daydreaming eyes, the action played out before me; the only verbal pressure I experienced the rapid unfurling of sentence after sentence, page after page, as fast as my fingers could write.

One of the older nurses in the hospital during my commitment had tried to tell me something once, though I had been too drugged and paranoid to understand her at the time. She had tried to cheer me by saying that "we manics" bore some special gifting. She'd taken on a confiding, almost conspiratorial tone. She said we were able to get things done; we had a certain kind of energy other people didn't. At the time, in my delirium and insanity, I thought she was telling me, like Professor X, that I bore some secret power, and that one day I might learn to harness it—the typical backstory of a comic book character or some mutant-cum-superhero. But later I would have occasion to wonder if that fire in the mind had something to do with what she meant, if she'd meant my weakness was also my strength, that every mountain casts, at times, a dark shadow.

And then I wondered how she knew that.

MY BALCONY WAS SO small I had to sit with my round charcoal grill at my elbow, close enough to be mistaken, at a distance, for some companion droid rather than an appliance for cooking meat. My view was one of commercial rooftops, expansive and flat. The tenant before me had left a word magnet stuck to the iron railing, a single-word poem that I decided summed up the city perfectly: MATERIALISTIC. I never removed it.

The most inspirational thing I could see, besides a few trees and two lofty radio towers, was the high arch of the Texas Star, a two-hundred-foot Ferris wheel on the state fairgrounds, a monstrous and skeletal structure even larger than the fiery disc that rose every morning beside it, as though even the sun itself were a thing Texans were ambitious to replace.

Closer by, in the immediate foreground, was an alley, a loading dock, and a dumpster that I began to think of, the longer I observed them, as a deceptively plain and unassuming stage where various human dramas were enacted. The loading dock was used most frequently as a smoking block for the skinny jean-clad employees of an animation and film effects studio. I watched them assume various postures. The story teller used his hands, gesturing coolly with his cigarette. They flicked spent filters to the pavement and swiped their key cards to return to the building. I watched an emo couple wander into the alley from the bars in Deep Ellum. They took out a paint pen and tagged the dumpster, then took a picture of themselves posing by it. A homeless man visited the dumpster regularly, climbing through the sliding door and ripping open bags of garbage the way I'd previously thought only bears did. I watched him uncap a gallon jug of milk and sniff it. Wadded food wrappers he unfolded, devouring crusts of bread and discarded pickles. He tipped his head back to drain the remnants of a soda bottle.

Once, I even entered the scene myself. I made a sandwich in my kitchen for the homeless man, got in my jeep, drove down through the parking garage and out through the apartment complex's security gate, winding through Deep Ellum until I found the alley and pulled up beside the dumpster. But by that time the homeless man had disappeared and the police were there. They gave me a wise look that said Don't bother, kid. They said they'd taken that particular man to the jail so many times for vagrancy that even the jail would no longer accept him. He was, I suppose, as close to a human bear as they have in the city limits.

I watched the police detain him at the dumpster once, stepping warily and giving him commands at arm's length, the partner positioned at a right angle to the man with his hand on his gun belt. The homeless man went through the ritual wearily, not looking at their faces. It was all a dance he had known once but no longer had any desire to perform. In the end, the officers snapped his picture with a digital camera, got in their cruiser, and left him to shoulder his backpack and wander away so slowly as to defy the very concept of pursuit.

I often brought my legal pads out to the balcony and mapped out stories, sun tan oil wicking into the ruled pages and finger smudges staining the cardboard backing. Inside, I printed out chapters and laid them side by side across the carpet, and across the seats of my couch, examining the sequence, interposing b-story scenes, building to a climax across multiple narrative threads, learning to hold an entire novel in my mind at once.

All my beginnings were there. Most of the stories and books I write, to this day, are the ones that began in seed form in that apartment: late-night scrawl in Moleskine notebooks, sprawling legal-pad mind maps, hand-written journal entries, stories pounded out on an overheated laptop, sometimes not leaving the apartment for days on end, eating cereal for most meals, only to emerge at last, nearly staggering, the world—the real world—an overwhelming assault on my narrowed senses.

I frequented the Half Price Books on Northwest Highway, scouring the shelves of the writing section for the sorts of volumes I would have been assigned if I'd been enrolled in a creative writing program. I discovered Noah Lukeman and John Gardner and read every book by them I could find. One of Gardner's admonitions I have never forgotten: make your sentences clear as a grizzly bear standing in a brightly lit kitchen.

I submitted short stories and poems to literary magazines and checked the little aluminum mailbox in the common area daily for rejection slips. I found plenty. No matter, Jack London had famously acquired more than six hundred rejections in a five-year period. I was in good stead.

I distinctly remember the afternoon I finished my first novel. I printed it out—nearly an entire ream of paper. I tapped the warm pages into a neat, tight stack with immense satisfaction, set it on the desk by the computer where I had written it, and looked at it admiringly. That first manuscript seemed to have a potent physical presence, an urgent reality, as though I had birthed something live or built a hydrogen bomb.

I crossed the apartment and stood at the window. Same scent of dust from the blinds. Same cars moving slowly on the elevated freeway barely visible in the distance. The world didn't know it yet, but I'd done something. I almost expected to hear a knock at the door. I fantasized about posing for dust jacket photographs down in Deep Ellum, standing in three-quarter pose against some graffitied brick wall: sophisticated, urbane, my face cloaked in appropriately authorial shadows. Black and white or color, though? Difficult decisions had to be made.

This was the novel—a sixty-page portion of it, at least—that had raised the eyebrows of someone in the seminary faculty. Apparently the majority of future pastors don't write supernatural thrillers in which an unnamed man that might be God passes bodily through solid motel walls and slays sex traffickers *in flagrante* with something that was either a light saber or an angelic sword.

I thought it was pretty cool.

To be fair, I'd actually wrestled quite a bit with the problem of evil in my novel. I was disturbed by the extent to which I was required to dwell in the scenes I wrote, lingering until I began to feel tainted by them. Some of those scenes I'd written in tears. In the sixty-page portion submitted for my Trinitarianism project, the unnamed man with godlike powers drives across the desert battling drug-runners and seeking to redeem a prostitute trapped in a miserable existence of slavery. It was intended to illustrate the Trinity in crisis, the effort of God to redeem humankind from the bondage of sin, to draw him into the inner life of the Trinity, only to find that the prodigal would rather return to her chains. It was Jürgen Moltmann meets Nicholas Cage. Apparently the professor, or perhaps his grader, hadn't quite appreciated some of my more subtle nuances.

The watch list was, I presume, for troubled students, those falling behind in their grades, appearing on campus in black trench coats, or found to be ordering bomb components via the internet. The thing that offended and disappointed me was that no one had even reached out to me. I might have scoffed if they had. I might have told them, in a huff, that the most amateurish interpretation of fiction possible is to assume its content to be unavoidably autobiographical.

Maybe I had gone too far. One day, after a class in church history, I approached the professor I believed to be the most sagacious on campus. I'm not sure why I thought he would have any opinions about fiction writing. The man had double-earned doctorates, though; he had to know nearly everything. Feeling a little foolish, I explained my situation as a writer and asked if he thought it was worth the offense, unpleasantness, and even *contamination* to depict actual, realistic evil in a work of fiction.

I was worried he wouldn't understand.

He smiled in a grandfatherly way and regarded me through the gleaming lenses of his bifocals before opening his mouth and gracing me with the oracular, eleven-word epiphany I had apparently come all that way to hear.

"Take the rocks out of the river," he said, "and it won't sing."

He shut his briefcase and I nodded.

In the end, I wandered away from seminary like I'd wandered away from plenty of other things in my life: uncertain, disturbed, inchoate, seizing upon problems that were really only excuses, spinning explanations in which financial problems were always more significant than my fundamental lack of personal clarity. In retrospect, the narrative I constructed about leaving seminary was far simpler than the reality.

I didn't belong there. I never officially dropped out; I simply stopped making payments and didn't register for the next term. If I ever set foot on campus again, I don't recall it. To my knowledge, none of the faculty ever made any inquiry as to what had happened to me. I was, I suppose, a problem that had solved itself.

✳ ✳ ✳

I GOT A JOB working in the fitness center of the Baylor University Medical Center, which had the benefit of extending the free membership I'd enjoyed as a student. My job title was "Fitness Instructor," and I even looked the part, but all we really did, as my manager liked to say, was "sling keys." The ranks of oak lockers in the men's and women's dressing rooms each had a corresponding brass key with an engraved brass octagon bearing its number, blue elastic wrist bands for the men and red for the women. My job, along with several others at the front desk, was to check members in, print out vouchers for personal training sessions, process payments for childcare, and swap out locker keys for gym ID cards—and sometimes their Mercedes key fob, their cell phone, or even a Jaeger-LeCoultre watch, which one member insisted I wear on my wrist while he worked out.

The back of the fitness center opened into a fenced-in park with a walking path that looped around a nice (but obviously man-made) pond, and in the center of the park was a little hill crowned with live oaks and a gazebo, stone slab steps leading up to it. A thousand miles from Cove Mountain, I used to worry that city living and all those cable machine work-outs were gradually robbing me of the peculiar fitness required to climb up to my old haunts. Sometimes I would go out to the park and run those evenly-placed stone steps, again and again, until a strange sort of homesickness came over me and the disparity became almost painful.

Unlike the little hill in the park, there are places on Cove Mountain where the terrain becomes so vertical that iron rungs have been installed in the rock face and the white blaze of the Appalachian Trail is painted on the rock beside them as if to say, Yes, we're not kidding; this is the way. I have watched many day hikers—sometimes with children or dogs—stop at these rungs, a stunned look on their faces as though some inherent contract with the Forestry Department had been violated. "How are we supposed to get up that?" they protest. Awkward dog relays would ensue, passing, from one set of hands to another, an elderly and man-handled retriever whose grimacing face and baleful eyes bespoke its shame.

I went back into the gym, watching men watch themselves in mirrors doing reps, a kind of work that vanished the instant they stepped away from the machine or racked their dumbbells. I watched women on treadmills: striding striding striding, ponytails bobbing, sometimes running as though they believed they could actually attain the profile of the starlet pictured in the open *People* magazine spread on the control panel before them.

I worked everyday from one until ten p.m., making good use of those long mornings to finish my novel and get in a workout before my shift started. It was there, standing attentively behind the front desk on the hard granite floor of the lobby that my manager, during a slow moment, showed me the BBC video of the Cordyceps fungus that turned ants into its brainwashed hosts, making them climb as high as possible before they died, scattering lethal spores to the wind.

"Dude," he said in a low voice, scanning the lobby for patrons, "what if this spread to humans? *That's* the book you should write!" I grinned and everyone we pitched the idea to grinned as well, because, of course, it was a crazy idea.

I continued to be a part of the social life of the seminary by means of the gym, where students were constantly coming and going. The members of my writers group came through. Doctors and lawyers stopped to chat with me once I memorized their names, sometimes dispensing expert advice for some aspect of a short story I was writing. Vietnam veterans told me stories. Cougars hit on me, inviting me to join their hot yoga class. Gay men brought me salads. Except for rush hour, when we defended the front desk like the Alamo, it really was an enjoyable free-for-all, a constant parade of fiction-inspiring characters. Dr. Charles Ryrie was one of my favorites, stooped and elderly, but incongruously clutching, in his arthritic fingers, the pair of red speedos he always wore while swimming laps. "When you get to be my age," he liked to say, "you don't buy green bananas!"

I continued to maintain the fantasy that I might meet someone at the gym, the way I'd hoped to find "one of those cute Texas girls," when I'd first moved to Dallas. I maintained an almost superstitious belief in Providence, always analyzing the circumstances under which I met someone, searching for a sign that it was meant to be. I believed, with all my heart, in the origin stories couples told. Mine was an incurable Romanticism rooted in the soil of a Calvinistic worldview. "Faith," I wrote in my journal, "is a practice of interpretation and a posture of storytelling. It continually imagines telling future stories to my grandkids about how I met my wife, how it just barely happened, how the circumstances demonstrated his unmistakable providence."

In my mind, it wasn't enough to simply hit things off with someone after meeting at a bar. I relished the tales of accidentally spilled coffee at a ski lodge, of chance meetings on elevators and nearly missed flights; if I began talking to another seminary student because she was late to class and the seat beside me just happened to be the last one available—well, there might be something to that. I'd given up entirely on the idea of online dating. "I need," I wrote, "a providential arrangement. Could I just turn around and meet some girl that wouldn't ruin my life, but would be a part and parcel of my deliverance?"

I remembered finding a long-tailed Luna moth on the fence outside our house one morning as a child. That moth was so misplaced, such an otherworldly part of the night, that my father said God had sent it for me. My most beloved retriever, too, had come to me as though sent, a stray I turned to find staring at me. This was the Providence that had a magical ring to it, the Providence that appointed a fish to swallow Jonah, the God who makes winds his messengers and flaming fire his ministers. In a strangely prophetic journal entry, I wrote, "Providence gifts us with otherworldly delights, sends them from the deeps to swallow us, from the depths of the forest to delight us, from wandering to join us;

the Lord instructs them and they come to us, emerge from the thicket where we would go blind with searching."

I did not, that year, find the love of my life. Providence was indeed at work, but not in any of the ways I had anticipated. I developed a painful case of plantar fasciitis, apparently from standing long periods behind the desk at the gym. I saw a podiatrist at the hospital, who told me I needed either physical therapy or surgery. Neither was exactly an option. I started looking online at pictures of shoes with springs on the heels—that's how bad it was. I developed a routine of coming home after my shift and plunging my feet into an ice bath for as long as I could stand it.

Orthopedic inserts, icepacks, stretching routines: nothing really worked. Even people that didn't know me well began to say I looked drained. The funny thing was I could still walk, run, and hike. It was as though I was allergic to standing still, as though someone was trying to tell me it was time to move on. I could only conclude that a season of my life was being forced to a close. I would have to either find another job or terminate the Texas experiment and boomerang my way back to Virginia. Neither of those options would get me any closer to the financial independence I craved. Despite the full-time hours I worked at the gym, my parents were still supplementing my income, and I was only making minimum payments on my credit cards, gradually accumulating debt.

I interviewed for a job running a painting business for a couple of wealthy entrepreneurs, the sort of men who had immigrated to America with nothing but the shirts on their backs and now drove Lamborghinis. Nothing came of it; I'd actually been shocked at the business practices they'd described, which could only be called cutthroat.

I applied for a job as a medical equipment sales rep, and spent long hours scrolling through online job boards. I was, in many ways, still working my way through the checklist of accomplishments my psychiatrist had said I'd never achieve. Even though I still had bouts with depression, I'd proven that I could live without antidepressants. I'd also proven that I could live by myself within four walls and continue to observe normal circadian rhythms. Now I needed to demonstrate some self-sufficiency and get a job and get married—happily if possible.

In June, I turned in my notice at the fitness center, despite having no definite plans. It is still hard for me to remember the luxury of such spontaneity. All I knew was that something had to change. I wrote a single journal entry that month, then didn't touch it again until August. It was a Saturday night. I could hear rooftop bands playing down in Deep Ellum, someone revving a chopper outside Reno's. My apartment was so quiet I could hear my pen scratching across the page. Four years had passed since I'd been with a woman.

"I'm trying to be good," I wrote. "I'm trying to live authentically, honestly, without any more regrets. I'm trying to please the Lord with my life, I'm trying to do what I think he wants me to. I keep waiting. Waiting for God to show up in my life with some kind of deliverance, some kind of relief... I keep thinking that these are supposed to be the best years of my life, and I have this sense of something getting away from me... It's hard to imagine how the next life will compensate for the one passing me by... What is the point of it all—the purpose, the vanity of a life? I'm getting ready to turn out the lights on one more day, and I'm not going to pretend to be able to tell you the answer."

THAT SUMMER WAS ONE of incredible and unexpected privilege. I spent three weeks back home hiking all my old trails, ruminating atop Dragon's Tooth, breathing in the mountain air like a healing elixir. Then I received an unexpected email. The opportunity for adventure had arisen: I was invited to join Joel and two other seminary friends at his parents' house in Kenai, Alaska for two weeks that August. All I had to do was get there. It was exactly the sort of adventure I needed. I flew back to Dallas at the end of the Alaskan summer with the scent of campfires on my clothes, acid stains on my arms from bushwhacking, a bag full of candied salmon, and more than fifteen hundred digital pictures on my camera.

Once I unpacked and had time to think, I decided to move back to Virginia if I didn't have a job offer by October. I relished the idea of ditching the city for the mountains, but I also anticipated the sense of defeat I'd have moving in with my parents at age twenty-nine. I'd have to pay a significant fee to break the lease on my apartment; I'd have to rent a moving truck and drive over a thousand gas-guzzling miles; and worst of all, I'd be limping home with nothing more than fifteen thousand dollars in credit card debt and an unpublished novel to show for the last two years of my life.

One of the friends from seminary that had gone to Alaska with me, Scott, (known as "the Wolf" after our wilderness adventures) had worked his way through seminary at an inspection services company in north Dallas that liked to hire Christian students. He said he would put in a good word for me, and that the company would probably appreciate my experience in construction, since the majority of their work consisted in looking at pictures of houses being built. I applied and had an interview ten days later. I shaved, donned one of the same business casual outfits I'd worn to seminary classes, and presented myself in a boardroom that overlooked the Preston and 635 area of north Dallas—what was, if you'd like to imagine it, essentially the setting for the movie *Office Space*, which had been filmed only a few miles away.

I looked out over the cubicle farm, trying to imagine leaving my jeep in a parking garage everyday, riding the elevator up to work, mug of coffee in hand, exchanging pleasantries with coworkers, idling in the break room, filling out TPS reports. Except for my stint at the gym, I'd never had a job that didn't involve a pickup truck and mud on my boots. Best of all, at least at first, was the thought that I'd be *sitting*, and my plantar fascia would have time to heal.

My future bosses had copies of my resume on the table, and flipping through it, they asked me a number of questions about the particular order in which a house is built: which comes first after framing: plumbing, mechanical, or electrical? They seemed perfectly satisfied with my answers and gave each other a subtle nod. They offered me forty-thousand dollars a year to sit in a cubicle. I was stunned. We shook on it and I began the next morning.

I left the office after my first day feeling like a zombie after staring at a computer screen for eight hours, but I was being well-compensated and could finally write in my journal that "I have the satisfaction of knowing I am a man who can handle his own problems." At last, I could consider myself a man. It was the end of an excruciatingly long adolescence. Now, if I was smart and conservative with the money I was making, I could not only support myself, but quickly pay off my debts. I knew I wasn't the type to sit in a cubicle for the rest of my life, but for now it was an answer to prayer. I also couldn't help but think of it as the corresponding punishment, in a karmic sort of way, for the crime of living in a fictional world for the past year. I had, in some way, violated the basic economic and mathematical realities of the universe, and so it only seemed fair that all the luxuries and privileges I'd enjoyed would bring about a day—or in this case, perhaps a year or two—of reckoning.

"So," I wrote, "I sit every day in a gray cubicle, and I think of it as something to be endured, a sentence that will last a certain number of years and then I will be released, and feel the sun on my face and the width of the open blue sky, and love it as only a freed man ever could."

TAKE ME AS A cautionary tale, if you will. Join me in wondering how, after every advantage I'd been given, I could have gone on to make the decisions I did; whether it meant that everything that came before—all my talk of God and the mysterious Providence directing my life—was nothing but sham and a pretense, or if, when a man is utterly alone, the weakness of a single moment is sufficient to wreck him.

For me, that moment came sitting on the end of the bench press, resting between sets. I'd talked to her plenty of times before, but that night was different. After I'd gotten the new job, my friends from seminary had gradually and variously departed: drifting back to their hometowns, rejoining their families, applying for jobs, figuring out the next chapter of their lives. I settled into a mind-numbing routine in my cubicle, sipping coffee and scrolling through photos of building projects, verifying stages of completion for the lending process, offering meaningless consultations based on my previous career in construction. Even my Saturday morning writer's group had devolved into a sort of breakfast club—an enjoyable and sometimes raucous group of friends—but no longer a gathering of serious writers.

I had been single too long. My own eligibility was a thing I suffered, sometimes keenly. When I worked at the gym, one of the older members, wistful and balding, had once leaned against the counter and asked if he could borrow my body on a Friday night to go pick up girls. Another night I kindly refused the proposition of an older but not-unattractive woman only minutes before the gym closed and we departed singly to our homes, cold and dark. I wrote in my journal that the absence of a woman in my life had become as tortuous as a constant level of physical pain. In my frustration and over-education, I sometimes entertained the dangerous notion that society at large was, to some extent, to blame for my singleness; that even in primitive societies, by my age, arrangements would have simply been made—nature would have been provided for, whether or not the impossible modern standard of a soul mate with perfect compatibility could be satisfied.

The thought that occurred to me that night—the night of a super moon, as it happened—after too much unguarded eye-contact with a beautiful woman, was *Why not? Why not do something to make your life easier?* Where that sibilant whisper had come from, or how ancient and original had been its appeal, was not something I was then wise enough to consider.

Here the convention of memoir runs afoul of perceived libel and unwanted publicity, particularly in this instance, since the woman in question, who would become my lover within the week, already enjoyed a certain degree of social status due to her intelligence and education, a status which has doubtlessly redoubled by the time of this writing, though to be honest, I never heard of her again after the year we spent together.

The details of a love affair are neither as significant or uncommon as one might suppose. Setting out to describe it, one would lapse, invariably, into pornography or else idolatry. Many fine novels have been written if you wish to have the vicarious experience of falling in love, of champagne and lovemaking, of all else abandoned, of bread eaten in secret, of oaths made of a night without token or witness but God. *Farewell to Arms* was the novel I imagined I was living at the time, so much so that when I finally left her I had the audacity to borrow a line of Hemingway's prose for the note I left behind: "We have a good time, don't we?"

Our breakup was the inevitable end of a disastrous year. It was such a perfect disaster, in fact, that I began to see in it something orchestrated, timed, and choreographed to perfection, like explosions in a war movie. These misfortunes were not coincidental; I knew my life was being judged. My Christian friends and family had accepted the many explanations I offered for our mutual living arrangement, explaining that we would be married at the courthouse right away, as soon as we could both get a coinciding day of vacation. Moving in together was only an unfortunate necessity due to financial pressures. In no way did I intend to circumvent the institution of marriage; I simply found myself in the first legitimate situation in which it might be violated.

Strangely, no one called me on it. But God is not mocked. I might escape the flames myself, but all my works of stubble and straw were about to be consumed. Like Jonah, I knew the storm had been sent for me. And like that far-flung prophet, I was not yet repentant, only bitterly sorry I had not managed to outrun the discipline of God.

A week before I left my fiancé, I wrote in my journal, "Why not quit resisting destruction and let it have its perfect result? Let it sweep my entire life with fire and see what remains, what rises from the ashes. Who can resist the hand of God? Again, I find myself a Jonah in an ocean full of waves. Come fish, swallow me down. Witness for me, you pagans, the perfect destruction of my life."

That year had begun with the most ambitious effort I'd ever made to advance myself as a writer. My first novel, far from saving me, had thus far only earned me eight agency rejections. Realizing an MFA in creative writing was the degree I needed, and after bemoaning (not for the first time) my useless degree in philosophy, I strategized that I could take several continuing adult education courses in creative writing at Southern Methodist University and possibly make the connections I'd need for letters of recommendation to grad school. It was a long shot, but I took it, sneaking out of work early on the evenings I had class, cursing traffic on 635, and eating dinner off my lap on the way to campus.

The program culminated, not in a degree, but in an expensive and tantalizing trip to New York City to meet in-person with agents and editors who were guaranteed to have read a sample of my manuscript and would be ready to offer feedback, and just perhaps, for the lucky few, an offer of representation.

The thing about writers is that we all, of necessity, believe we are the exception to the rule. You could tell a group of one hundred writers that the only thing in the way of fame and publication was a dip in shark-infested waters, and furthermore that ninety-nine percent of them would perish in the attempt, and every one of them would enter the water believing they were destined to be the sole survivor. I was no different.

The fee for the three-day conference was prohibitive, and wildly presumptuous given the ever-diminishing advance a first-time author could expect during a recession economy. I was never any good at playing poker for this same reason: I couldn't resist pushing all my chips forward. I was the *one*, in a Kung-Fu movie kind of way. Odds could be overcome. I was purchasing a lottery ticket. Or would, if I could find the money.

Oddly enough, my father volunteered to pay my way, which stunned me because all my life he'd been a hard-bitten realist about the chances of my making it as a professional writer. I'd never realized his cynicism was directed at the world, not me; that when it came down to it he believed in his son and loved what his son loved, even to the point of financing one of the craziest gambles I ever took.

It took going back and rereading my journals more than a decade later to understand why, with no one actually pushing me, I had voluntarily raised the stakes so high for my success, and why I had decided it had to happen so suddenly, that year. I now realize how desperately, if subconsciously, I was attempting to mitigate the vast inequality between my fiancé's profession and my own. While I was sitting in a cubicle she was literally saving people's lives, and in order to continue to play the man for her I would have to at least approximate, in my career, the accomplishments she'd made in hers. Even if my efforts didn't produce an immediate windfall of cash, I at least needed to be recognized as showing great promise, of being on track to perform among the top ten percent of my peers. I needed my story to be proportionately epic to hers.

In plenty of other careers, a year of hard work might have accomplished that.

I BOARDED THE PLANE, found my seat, and set to work on my latest bit of fiction: a text message to my boss about a sudden bout of vomiting and fever. Conveniently, Swine Flu had been a big scare that year, and the symptoms I reported were disturbingly similar. I would, I assured him, see a doctor as soon as possible and report back.

It's hard to imagine many of the other passengers who landed at La Guardia that afternoon being as anxious about the Big Apple as I was. In the preceding months I'd noticed my hair visibly graying. I'd started carrying around a bottle of Pepto-Bismol everywhere I went, taking hits off it the way an alcoholic nurses a hidden flask. Many nights I'd bolt upright from sleep when acid reflux crept into my throat. Everything I ate had begun to taste like ash. My heart sometimes fluttered. At a routine doctor's visit my blood pressure had been 130/80, what medical professionals typically consider stage-one hypertension. I was thirty years old.

I found New York City to be like stepping onto the set of a movie. The air was cool and the leaves of the old trees along Fifth Avenue were yellowed and drifting on the breeze into Central Park. I was staying in the upper eastside at the House of the Redeemer, an old Italianate mansion on 95th, only a short walk down 5th Avenue to the Guggenheim and the Met, where an a cappella quartet was performing outside the museum, perhaps a hundred people sitting on the steps listening, while street vendors hawked panoramic photos of the city and copies of Broadway Scripts, pedestrians stopped to buy hot dogs or paused to sip coffee, and other passerby walked enormous dogs—Newfoundlands and Labradors that practically dragged their owners across the street toward the trees, releasing great streams of piss that ran down the bark and puddled in the street, and all the while taxis honked and waves of pigeons rose: all directed, it seemed to me, by an unseen cinematographer.

But it was real, and I was really there, living out a dream, making my big move, about to sit across from the very agents and editors that had previously been as inaccessible to me as pixies and unicorns. Of course it didn't work. My first novel, if brilliant, was apparently of that particular species of brilliance for which the New York literary world was unprepared.

"It's complicated," an editor from Penguin sighed. "*Too* complicated." She grilled me with questions for fifteen unpleasant minutes.

"Who *are* all these people?" another agent asked about my characters.

Wasn't it obvious they were fallen angels? Apparently not.

"It's very *cinematic*," a film agent said. "Call me once you have a book deal."

"It's a very *ambitious* novel," another agent managed, and asked me to email him the full manuscript.

"If the rings in your story have magical properties," a book doctor advised, "they need to vibrate or emit a thin trail of smoke, something that signals they're part of the occult." For fifteen bucks a page he would be happy to fix all my manuscript's problems, adding, apparently, as many B-movies effects as he saw fit.

Even though my first novel was something of a block party for misfits, I left New York City with enough manuscript requests that I thought there was a good chance one of the agents would bite. Even the editor from Penguin had warmed up to me at a later dinner party, and after I'd regaled a table full of women with stories about bear attacks, she'd conferred upon me the honor of her business card, which is, if you don't know, kind of a big deal in those circles.

I rode back to Texas on a good tailwind, passing high and soundless over the wooded slopes of the Appalachians without thinking much of my old summits, certainly without imagining that in three months' time they would be the only refuge I knew. I took my fiancé out to dinner at a steakhouse, ordered a fifty-dollar bottle of wine, and laid out the agents' business cards on the starched white tablecloth for her to examine, as though they were souvenirs from a foreign country. She inspected them eagerly, fingering them for their thickness and the quality of the cardstock, impressed. All along, she had been just as excited as I was, and now it was real. My success seemed, in that moment, as likely to happen as it ever did. Any instant, an email might simply materialize in my inbox and change my life forever. Or not. But I refused to consider failure, or even the possibility of failure until the moment I face-planted in it. I would go down betting on that river card to the very last.

King Solomon wrote in the book of Proverbs that "hope deferred makes the heart sick," proving, despite scant archaeological evidence, that literary agents have existed from ancient times. My first day back within the gray walls of my cubicle I must have checked my email a hundred times. I daydreamed about an advance big enough to live on for a year while I wrote my next novel, perhaps even enough left over to buy a ring for my fiancé.

A week passed. Then two weeks. I became exhausted from the waiting, by the adrenaline rush and crash every time I checked my email and found nothing there. My parents reassured me it might take months to hear back—funny since everything they knew about literary agents they had learned from me. I kept waiting. I waited in my cubicle the way prisoners strain to hear the signal for a jailbreak or the way shipwreck survivors strain to hear the drone of a plane on the horizon.

Five days later, I received the first rejection. It was a polite but unflattering note from the agent who had deemed my novel "ambitious." He regretted that he was probably not the best agent for my work, best of luck placing it elsewhere, et cetera, nothing better than I'd gotten mailing query letters from home, really. I gathered from the agent's phrasing that he'd read no more than thirty or forty pages out of four hundred, and had completely missed the subtle nuances of my novel, the layers of symbolic meaning, to say nothing of the spiritual significance implied by fallen angels having gunfights. He still seemed to think it was "a crime noir detective story with a contemporary spin." The pathos of my literary work had been so badly misunderstood that for a moment I wondered if I'd received a rejection intended for someone else. That it might have been partly (read *fully*) my fault that no one knew what the hell my first novel was about was, of course, far from my consideration. It was simply so sophisticated a work that it was impossible to adequately summarize.

I did realize, at least, that the bubble was burst. The fantasy I had labored so hard to anchor in reality was slipping back into the dream world. It was not hard to imagine that more rejections would follow. New York agents would not be *competing* to represent me, as I had fantasized, like brokers waiving tickets at the Stock Market.

I waited an entire day before I told my fiancé.

The inevitable conversations that followed did not go well. "What if you never get published? What if you never succeed?" Neither of us actually voiced those questions, but they were obvious enough. We both grew miserable. Reality had to be faced. I had leveraged my remaining credit for a quick victory—dropping, for instance, a thousand dollars at Nordstrom on clothes for my trip when I was already badly in debt, and now I had nothing but a handful of swanky business cards to show for it. Not exactly the way I'd planned out the Hero's Journey.

My fiancé accused me of growing gray in the face. I couldn't have explained it then, but I must have sensed that the window for jump-starting my career had closed, the Hail-Mary-pass career method had failed. The development of whatever future I had as a writer could take years. *Years.* I didn't have years. My accumulated sins were like a credit card bill I would not dare to remove from the envelope, only tearing along the fold and prying it open with one finger. The minimum payment had become unsustainable. A major reckoning was at hand.

Another month passed without hearing from any of the agents, each silent day rendering my hope all the more ludicrous. About that time, nerve damage pain from my carpal tunnel suddenly worsened, with a new throbbing in my upper arm, to the point that I was barely able to function at work. My hands were cold to the touch and sluggish to obey. I struck the keyboard harder and harder to compensate until the joints in my fingers ached. At home, with numbness in my fingertips, I dropped a plate of cake, broke dishes in the sink, and fumbled to an embarrassing degree, my fork often falling loudly to the plate during meals. My fiancé opined, in disgust, that if we had a kid I would drop him on his head.

I went to see a surgeon and watched him examine my hands and arms, tapping here and there as though testing reflexes and noting when I felt an electrical jolt. He dictated the case as he went, activating the recorder with a foot pedal and turning his head as though speaking to someone invisible in the room.

"The patient is complaining of paresthesia in his right and left hands and shows Tinel's sign upon examination," he said.

Another doctor performed a nerve conduction study, hooking me up to electrodes, measuring my arm and marking it with ink like a carpenter preparing to cut a piece of lumber. He applied gel and used a two-pronged taser to send electrical currents into my nerves, what felt like being shocked on the old cow fence back home. Next came something like acupuncture needles stuck into the muscles of my arms and hands, and then they had me flex, measuring the activity of my nerves, which I noticed registering on their machines like a kind of static.

At the end of the study I asked the doctor if he could discuss the results with me informally, so I wouldn't have to wait in suspense until my next appointment with the surgeon, still some ten days off. The poor man could have hardly understood how quickly my life was unraveling.

I had, he said, mild to moderate carpal tunnel in my hands again and something new, too: my ulnar nerve, particularly in my right arm, was entrapped at the elbow, a fairly severe case of cubital tunnel, the nerves conducting at 37 meters per second instead of the usual 50-60. All the activities of a day, he explained, particularly repetitive motions at work, but also movements as innocent as reaching up to scratch one's nose, accumulate into repeated aggravation of the entrapped nerve, resulting in the throbbing, numbness, tingling, and loss of motor control I had experienced. Just imagine that your nerves are a rope and that the rope is being pulled through a fist that is gradually tightening and you'll have the idea, he said.

I knew exactly what he meant. The "Maestro," I wrote in my journal, was "poised over my life, wand cradled expertly in his hands, hair a fury of movement and his eyes closed with the passion of directing disaster upon disaster like cymbal clashes in some discordant bar of the tragic symphony that was my life."

✷ ✷ ✷

AFTER I TOLD MY boss I could no longer type, I was left to sit in my cubicle for nearly an entire week without assignment or instruction. I came in to work, day after day, drank coffee, and sat staring out the window or listening to Coldplay via my earbuds. I became an unspoken pariah, my bosses emerging suddenly from their offices, casting what seemed to be involuntary glances, gopher-like, across the cubicle farm in my direction before disappearing behind other closed doors for meetings, the subject of which I could only assume included this strange new problem. I had the distinction of being the first employee of that company to ever file for worker's compensation.

It wasn't going to work, of course, but my doctor had even put it in writing, declaring my job duties to be a direct cause of the problem, and I figured, wrongly, that a surgeon's word would be worth quite a bit in court. What I would have needed for a good case, I later learned, was for one of my bosses to drop a filing cabinet repeatedly on my head while at least two other employees witnessed it, one of whom was a saint and the other a Notary Public.

My workload had gradually increased since I was hired, my job morphing entirely, due to the recession, from reviewing online draw inspections to generating feasibility studies from scratch, a process that consisted, almost entirely, of data entry. Coworkers from adjacent workspaces occasionally poked their heads over the top of my cubicle wall to see what in the world I was doing to my keyboard. "You're going to set that thing on fire," they'd say. Eight or nine months had gone by since I had requested a typing assistant. No one, I was told, could be spared to assist me.

Since the numbness in my hands began, I had made numerous attempts to abate the problem, buying a special ergonomic keyboard, my coworkers at first saying "Ergo-what?" sounding like confused Cartesians, before they settled on the apparently

Texan form of the word, pronouncing it ERA-GOMIC. I bought various alternative trackpads and trackballs and mice, but still my symptoms worsened. I had, by that stage, reached such a point of inflammation that nothing short of moving the cursor on the screen with my mind would have helped. The CFO of the company visited my cubicle and quipped that we might have to try to get a hospital bed for me to work from. I was not amused.

My sleep became increasingly disturbed, waking in the night with my upper arm throbbing and the lower portion of my arms and hands numb, unable to move my middle, ring, and pinky fingers—the fingers enervated by the ulnar nerve, I learned. My fiancé mocked me for the braces I began to wear to bed, my arms bound by splints and Velcro straps from my armpits to my fingers, rendering me rigid and inflexible as a mannequin lying beside her.

Filing for worker's comp had been like pulling the pin on a grenade. Not exploding it, but simply holding it in my fist like a terrorist. Had I known the goat-rope I was initiating, I would have simply laughed and walked away from it all. But I had the irrational hope, even at that late stage, that I might pull my life out of the nosedive it had taken. My bosses became strangely aloof, sitting stone-faced in the meetings we held, meetings in which I attempted to explain how my symptoms had worsened and what had been the doctor's prognosis.

They offered little sympathy. They said they would schedule an ergonomics expert to come analyze my workspace to see what "reasonable accommodation" could be made, as though this were all a simple matter of comfort and not a medically serious injury. It was clear they had already been speaking to attorneys. Several times my immediate supervisor had called me into vacant offices to explain, rather perfunctorily, my legal rights relating to contacting a case worker—the kind of information always laminated and posted prominently in the employee break area, but the last sort of thing anyone ever expects to actually need.

When I'd first taken the job, I'd been offered disability insurance for an additional fee every month, but at the time I'd shrugged it off, hardly able to imagine how I could be injured sitting around in dress clothes, clicking a mouse, and riding elevators to lunch. I used to be the construction superintendent that was sent to tell a bunch of ex-cons brandishing nail guns that they weren't getting paid that Friday because the house wasn't finished. This office gig was the cushiest—and seemingly the safest—job I'd ever had.

Of course, none of it was their fault. Not really. I'd brought the problem with me; it was within me, this weakness, like a genetic defect or the consequences of original sin; latent, a fate overtaking me, that massive fish trailing the boat like a shadow, waiting for the storm, waiting for the splash. All this was only teaching me why the book of Jonah had been written as a satire.

I sat in my cubicle that last week, fully expecting to be fired. One night, over hamburgers and beers at the Angry Dog in Deep Ellum, I told Heath Coles, one the friends I'd been to Alaska with, that I was "watching them build the gallows." Once they'd brought in the ergonomics expert—likely to be a character straight out of *Office Space*—they'd have the paper trail they needed to demonstrate in court that they'd made "every reasonable accommodation" for the problem that would, in the end, be deemed not a workplace injury, but only a "condition of life." For crying out loud, they already had me training my replacement, which made the whole thing about as obvious as tumbling out of a van in the desert and being tossed a shovel.

My replacement was more like one of the roughnecks I used to work with than the office types around us, seemingly content to pass their days in a cubicle under fluorescent lights. They had hired men like us for the risk management department because we had actually spent most of our life in the field, and could look at a picture of a construction site and tell if something was hokey. My replacement came to work every day wearing a leather jacket with a giant eagle patch sewn to the back of it, its talons grasping bundles of arrows and spears, and various other patches that declared "Proud to be an American" and "Live to Ride." I watched him hover over the keyboard, one finger extended from each fist, hunting and pecking his way through the phrases we used to the point of absurdity: Cost appears adequate Cost appears adequate

Cost appears adequate, cutting and pasting as much as possible. We were, after all only making reports for the bank's renovation lending process. Problems arose if we actually used our construction knowledge to notate problems, such as, God forbid, "DISCONNECTED WIRES FROM STOLEN AIR CONDITIONING UNIT APPEAR TO POSE ELECTROCUTION HAZARD," one of my more enjoyable moments of marginalia, unfortunately deleted after my boss received a phone call.

You see, the banks didn't *really* want to know about potential problems with a loan, which was, ironically, one of the very reasons the world had been plunged into a recession. But never mind all that. I had a stack of completed reports piling up in a cubby over my desk nearly a foot tall, and I had promised myself that I would quit once they reached the top. In the meantime, I kept my creativity alive by sculpting dinosaurs from the foil wrappers of the burritos I ate for lunch. So far I had a tyrannosaurus rex, a triceratops, a brontosaurus, and one I was particularly proud of: a pterodactyl soaring midair, suspended by a length of dental floss I'd borrowed from a coworker.

Sometimes I just closed my eyes and imagined that the gray fabric walls of my cubicle were actually the cold gray rocks on the skyward summit of Cove Mountain. I'd been there so many times I could very nearly go there in my mind, could almost feel the rocks under my numb fingertips.

I had to stay in the office until six every evening to answer calls from the west coast, but during his training period, my replacement still left at five. He put on his leather jacket and flashed me the peace sign. Months before, I'd scored a cubicle next to the window, an uninspiring view of the parking lot that was nonetheless like looking out over Malibu Bay compared to a gray fabric cubicle divider.

Several stories down, I watched him walk to his motorcycle, a custom Harley Davidson chopper. He fired the engine, throttling it a couple times—ostensibly to warm it up, I'm sure—a throaty sputter and the whole bike vibrating, the side view mirrors trembling like the chrome antennae of some great and terrible urban insect. He lit a cigarette, hot-boxed it, then straddled the Harley and eased it out into the street like a pilot coming about on a runway. He gunned it, rocketing down the street, hands high on the raised handlebars, and the roar of the chopper setting off the alarm of a nearby luxury sedan.

There, at least, went a man the office could not harm.

HOW IT ALL ENDED with my fiancé, the insults that were spoken and the alcohol spilled and the cigarettes smoked down to burning remnants nearly extinguished by tears, is hardly worth relating.

By then only two places in the city felt remotely like home. One was my storage unit, where I sometimes went to sit on my old couch and think. The other was a coffee shop in Lakewood called Legal Grounds, where my writer's group had met during our best years, and where I still often went to write. I'd been friends with Cory, the owner, ever since the day her kitchen staff failed to show and I spent a Saturday morning washing dishes in exchange for a bottle of scotch. When I told Cory I'd decided to leave my fiancé, she handed me a scrap of receipt paper bearing the name and number of a friend that owned a moving company. I called them, and quite miraculously, they were able to come within hours, pulling up in a white eighteen-foot van emblazoned with the words PHOENIX EXPRESS SERVICES. I stared at that for a while.

I wept in every room of that apartment before it was over, but as for the point I drove home when my fiancé opened the door and saw nothing of me or mine but dimples in the carpet where my furniture had rested—

* * *

I LAY SHIVERING THAT night on an inflatable mattress, raft-like and adrift on a concrete floor that had been painted an aquatic blue. I was occupying the empty spare bedroom of the house where my friend Heath lived, cardboard boxes scattered around me like jettisoned cargo from the wreck that was my life.

Trouble was, the house did not actually belong to Heath, who leased his room from the man who owned the property, who was currently off traveling for business. Within a few days of moving in, word came from the owner that I would not, for whatever reason, be allowed to live in the house on a permanent basis, but neither would he turn me out into the street. I could stay for the remainder of the month, another three weeks. He did insist, however, that I be provided with a copy of his House Rules, one of which was to never touch the thermostat, set during winter on sixty degrees, and in summer at eighty.

I dressed in layers, donned a stocking cap and fingerless gloves, and wrote with numb fingers in my journal that the owner could "kiss my frozen ass." It did not occur to me at the time that this man I had never met now served as a proxy for God himself, He who owned the universe and had finally imposed his rules on my life: age-old rules of a cold and unchangeable order, the unyielding law that had brought me to ruin, that had made a mockery of my sham marriage, my ambition, and the brinkmanship I'd played with God, man, and a little organization called Citibank.

I imagined this owner to be fastidious and frugal, a tidy little man of sweater vests and clean eyeglasses, possessing no carnal appetites, off building a career and making investments of the type that had never even occurred to me. That he had gone into a far country and had left his house in the care of another, and that he would later return with a reckoning for those that disregarded his word—all this must have struck me, at a subconscious level, as maddeningly biblical.

I found myself in a Catch-22-type situation. I could not, after filing for worker's compensation, simply go out and get another job—even though there was plenty of work I might have been capable of—because, of course, the bare fact of my employment could be used in court to invalidate my injury, no matter how real and legitimate that injury might be. No one could see or measure my pain, but they could see me doing another job and perhaps they could even send a photographer to document my apparent lack of disability. It had been done before. In the upside-down world of disability claims, I was forced to be entirely disabled or not disabled at all.

I was afraid to be seen in public typing on my laptop, even though working on one of my short stories was nothing like the non-stop data entry that had injured me. I had never filed for worker's comp and didn't know how much paranoia was justified. Just to play it safe, for the next few weeks when I went to the coffee shop to kill time, I wrote longhand in one of my notebooks.

Certain signs, already, seemed to indicate that filing for worker's comp might turn out to be a huge mistake. I had already driven across town to the Texas Department of Insurance to fill out paperwork, (a DWC Form 041, if you want to know) waiting in a sparsely furnished waiting area that might have been the time capsule of a public defender's office from the 1980's. Several times, when I tried to call the local office to speak with my case manager, I was annoyed to find someone on the other end of the phone who seemed completely clueless, only to listen to them experience an epiphany moments later: "Oh, this is the Austin office. Where are you? Oh, you want to talk to someone in Dallas."

"I called the Dallas office," I insisted.

They helpfully provided me with the same number I'd just dialed.

I called again. Different voice, just as clueless.

"Oh, this is the San Antonio office," the new voice said. "Where are you? Oh, you need to call the Dallas office."

It was finally explained to me, at some point beyond exasperation, that if you called a local office that was busy, the call was simply bounced around Texas like an unwanted pinball until an available office picked up. I finally gave up and drove across town for every necessary communication.

The issue was whether or not I needed to stay in Dallas for a hearing before a judge, or if leaving town and heading back to Virginia might be an option. Either way, I had to figure it out before I overstayed my welcome at Heath's house. I was not heartened to find myself at the mercy of a handful of listless government bureaucrats. Already, the experience had an extremely negative feel to it, as though I were joining not just the ranks of the injured, unemployed, and disabled, but the Victim Class, for which apathy and inaction seemed the necessary prerequisites.

I was, during those weeks, as depressed as I have ever been. From the first night, my fiancé barraged me with notes and text messages begging me to come back, pleading with me to reconsider. I returned every night to my cold room, lying on that mattress full of chilled air. Why, the world seemed to ask, was I so determined to ruin the life I'd once enjoyed? I entertained thoughts of starting over, getting any job I could find and giving up on the idea of worker's compensation. The problem was, I really was injured. When I finally saw a surgeon, they described the four surgeries I would need: carpal tunnel release on both hands, and a more extensive surgery on each of my elbows with a lengthy incision and the possibility of losing as much as thirty percent of my triceps.

Picking up another job, whether it was washing dishes or sitting in yet another office, wasn't going to fix any of that miraculously. I sensed, even then, that some major lifestyle change would be necessary. This could take years.

As much to keep myself sane as to escape the cold, I drove to Legal Grounds most mornings for breakfast, eating blueberry pancakes and pouring myself into the short story I was writing as a form of distraction. Ironically, it was turning out to be one of the funniest pieces I'd ever done. Not ironically, the protagonist found himself in a house with no heat during a winter ice storm.

Legal Grounds was the kind of coffee shop that had a local reputation for its breakfast, and on Saturday mornings it was not uncommon for a line to stretch out the door, and even on week-days an informal system of social obligation existed such that few patrons dared to linger at their table once the plates were cleared away—not when the people standing in line were casting them looks made grim by low blood sugar.

I was the exception. Once my place had been cemented there, Cory had made it clear that I was to sit and write as long as I want-ed, but she did enjoy heckling me in front of the other customers (Oh my gosh, how long does it take to eat a couple of blueberry pancakes?) and sometimes we'd go on with a little exchange of impromptu dialogue, our tone rising like a couple of New Yorkers arguing over a parking spot, until people at nearby tables began to hide their faces behind their coffee mugs. I had become a fixture. I suppose if I'd stayed in that city and if that coffee shop had re-mained unchanged, there might have been, one day, in some cor-ner, a black-and-white photograph of me on the wall, or perhaps a little memorial plaque by the seat I usually occupied.

As long as I was there writing, refilling my coffee from the air pots under the trophy deer head mounted to the wall (Coffee un-der a buck, Joel had once quipped) I could immerse myself in a fictional world where everyone knew me, I had a place I belonged, and I had work to do that was meaningful and rewarding.

Afternoons, though, I had to face reality. Returning to the house and enduring the ennui of the remaining daylight hours nearly undid me. All my friends were at work, of course, living out their lives like normal people. I often sat and stared at noth-ing in particular, like some shell-shocked survivor. I would con-sider courses of action as simple as going to the grocery store and yet I could not bring myself to do it. Imagine spending a day in which it was against your doctor's better advice to use your hands or even bend your elbows and you'll get the idea. I could only write in my journal by taking frequent rests to relieve the fatigue caused by nerve damage in my arm and hand. I managed to write that I was "exhausted from floating around the city without any sense of permanence, looking at everything with a kind of itinerant mind-set; and everywhere, on every side-street and in every restaurant, in the grocery store, in the gym: vivid memories, most of them good and all of them cast in that strange sentiment of retrospect, even the worst of them lent a kind of bittersweetness."

I found out that my worker's comp claim had already been denied; but not to worry, the case worker told me cheerily, they deny everything at first. The tone of her voice seemed to imply I should consider this normal. Now I'd have to file an appeal with the Texas Division of Worker's Compensation Insurance (or something like that, the title so long that by the time it was over you forgot how it began) which would review my case and—if everything went right and David was able to defeat Goliath—*force* the insurance company to pay. Of course, even if I did win, I would only recover sixty-five percent of my lost income.

I hit a new low one morning after lying in bed too long listening to rainwater spattering in a thin, continuous thread against the gutter pan, and found I could not even summon the words to pray. My ex-fiancé had mentioned hanging herself in one of her recent letters. It is now hard to remember the hours I spent in tortured contemplation of my decisions, tossing on the air mattress, second-guessing and reasoning through every point of it again and again, trying to imagine another way but always arriving at the same, inescapable and devastating conclusion.

When I did manage to pray, I begged of God what unbelievers do when the sorry details of their lives overtake his history of miracles, prophecy, and revelation—even the advent of his Son as predicted by the stars. Blind to these, I asked for a sign. If only God could send some small encouragement, then perhaps I could summon the will to continue.

Later that afternoon, my mother called to tell me that she had just gotten a card in the mail from the mother of my best friend from childhood. I had been the best man at his wedding nearly ten years before but seldom talked to him now. His wife had just delivered his third son, my mother told me, and could I guess what they had named him? They had named him after me.

For a moment I couldn't speak, and then I sat on the stairs inside that empty house, held my fist to my mouth and wept. It was the strangest sort of encouragement I could have imagined. It was an undeserved dispensation of grace, entirely incongruous with my ruined life. It brought with it both a sense of accountability and shame. No one in their right mind would name a child after me. And yet, I thought, I might overcome these trials; I might change my life; I might become a better man—I might even become the sort of man that a little boy would not be ashamed to learn of one day.

When I couldn't stand the waiting any longer, I decided to move everything into my storage unit, go to Virginia for a visit, clear my head on a few mountaintops, and make yet another attempt to figure out life. Several times lately, I had found myself imagining the dark purple clouds on the horizon to be mountains. I doubt many people in that lowland city thought of mountains as being purple, but if they'd ever stood on the summit of Cove Mountain long after sunset and watched the blush fade from the sky and the hues of the forest deepen toward night, they would know, as I did, that they often were.

I called Phoenix Express Services again, and this time they showed up with a twenty-six-foot box truck. They backed it up to the front of the house, pulled a ramp down to the sidewalk, and rolled up the rear door. I gazed into the cargo area, cavernous and empty.

"This is a much bigger truck than last time," I said.

"Yeah," the owner of the moving company said, a wistful twinge to his voice, "we're getting ready to drive this up to Pennsylvania to load up my girlfriend's house and move her down here." Apparently she had just been laid off.

I stared at all that space. I was Jonah, standing at the mouth of the whale, being swallowed in slow-motion.

"Sure is a shame," he said, rehashing the concept as if it were a bit of heavy-handed dialogue from a screenplay, hitting the point right on the nose. "Shame to drive a big, empty truck all that way."

"You probably go up interstate 81, then, don't you?" I asked.

"Yeah, we'll take 40 over to 81, then it's a straight shot all the way."

"Right through Virginia."

"Yep."

Even then, I was too stubborn and blind to recognize what was happening. I told the owner I'd have to get a quote from him for moving me back to Virginia, since it was something I might be deciding on soon.

"Well, hell, why don't we do it now?" he said. What if, he proposed, instead of putting everything in my storage unit, we just loaded up everything from the unit as well, and he could drop it off in Virginia on his way to Pennsylvania?

I rubbed the back of my neck. I hadn't been prepared to make that decision when I woke up that morning. Perhaps God knew I never would without a hard nudge in that direction. But I-81 *did* run right through my hometown, within a few *miles* of my parents' house. Coincidences like this didn't just happen. God was making this painfully obvious.

A few minutes later, we shook hands on a deal that would move me back to Virginia for less than the cost of renting a truck myself, let alone the cost of fuel and the labor to load everything. The owner and his helpers fell to the work with the whistling cheerfulness of longshoremen, as though their lives had meaning again.

Thirty minutes earlier, I had not been moving back to Virginia; now I was. That's how fast it happened. One night later, another strange thing happened. A record snow fell, blanketing the Metroplex with nearly nine inches—more snow than the city had seen since 1917. I went for a walk that morning, taking in Dallas as I'd never seen it. Sheer purity covered the grime of the city like absolution. A few adventurous cars fishtailed in the streets. Everywhere, adults were acting like children, looking around wide-eyed, rolling up grassy-bottomed snowmen. Statues wore stovepipe hats of snow. Mexican kids scooped up huge clumps and flung them at each other, laughing, no clue how to pack a snowball.

"I searched for some sign in it," I wrote in my journal, "but the snow seems like a gift for the city itself, and my soul is too heavy, too tired to feel much relief, though it would in one of my stories. But life is not so well-constructed, and it is so hard to see the reason for things, so hard to tell the beginning from the end, hard to be the one being written instead of the one writing."

The movers called and said they'd be delayed in leaving town. I decided to stay in Dallas for two more weeks, ferrying paperwork back and forth between government offices as necessary and hoping for a quick resolution, hoping I wouldn't have to stay in town for a judicial hearing, and hoping I wouldn't lose my mind in the process.

I made the best of it. I bought a space heater for my room and stacked the few remaining cardboard boxes at the end of the air mattress like a headboard to keep my pillows from falling off during the night. One night, I lit all the pillar candles from my old apartment, the ones I used to have artfully arranged in the fireplace. I stared into the flames and for a while I watched scenes from my old life play before my eyes. "The open highway is there as soon as I am ready," I wrote in my journal, "and it leads into the distance as far as I want to go."

THOSE WEEKS OF LIMBO ended almost as suddenly as they began. Two weeks later, I received word that I would be permitted to attend my appeal hearing by conference call. I was finally free to go.

I said a number of good-byes. I even met my ex at a café and apologized for the sudden way I'd left. I tried to explain my reasons, why it would never work; I tried to bring a sense of rational closure to it, but for all our efforts it only resulted in more tears, violently shed, clinging to each other over the console of her car, nearly convulsing, nearly hyperventilating, and in the end I only left her again, weeping in her car in a parking lot. You can't look love in the face twice, as my friend Joel used to say.

The night before I left town, several of my friends remaining from seminary, Ryan Smith, Heath Coles, and J.D. Lemming met me for pints of Guinness and saucer-sized burgers at The Angry Dog. My favorite waiter, Vince, shook my hand and wished me well, and my friends raised their beers in my honor, and at the risk of waxing sentimental I wrote in my journal that "it was a good way to end things... laughing with the guys, just like so many good times, the best of times I had here..."

Cory refused to let me pay for my last breakfast at Legal Grounds, and sent me away with a logo-emblazoned coffee mug that I still use to this day. The morning before, in a rare display of emotion, she had packaged up a ridiculous number of muffins to sustain me on my trip. I remember watching her, how she transferred them, one by one, from the basket on the counter to a pair of open Styrofoam clamshells, how it seemed that she would never stop and how the whole time she seemed to be struggling to keep a brave face. The next time I came to Dallas and drove to Legal Grounds, the café would be gone.

I wound up taking the muffins downtown and giving them to the front desk staff at the Baylor Tom Landry Fitness Center, among whom I was now something of a legend because I had lobbied the director to allow us to sit on barstools when we weren't busy.

"This is the guy that got us the chairs!" they told the newbies. I sat in the lobby behind the huge brass eagle sculpture and played several games of chess with my old manager, Chris Brumley, knowing I would miss our conversations.

That last morning, I loaded the rest of my things into my jeep and, as an afterthought, hung the burrito-foil pterodactyl I'd kept in my cubical from the rearview mirror. I left the coffee shop after breakfast and slipped into my old apartment complex, past the security gate that doesn't really keep anyone out, and drove up to the top level of the parking garage and parked my car and walked over to the rail and looked out over Deep Ellum, like looking over the rail of a ship. I remembered how wild and unknown it had all seemed when I first moved in, how frightening and full of potential, how sex and destiny and perhaps even death or the Devil himself had come to me like scents on the hot wind, how timid I'd been, how little I'd known of the city, how my parents had been afraid for me—even at six-foot-three and looking like a former football player—to walk the sidewalks alone.

I counted the chimneys across the rooftop to my old apartment, where all my changes had been. It seemed more fitting somehow, that I should drive away from this spot, where it had first begun, where my home had rightfully been, where, if I had been wiser, I might have yet remained. But none of that now could ever be known.

I departed the city by the exact same route I had entered: Gaston to Carroll, Carroll to Interstate 30. At the entrance ramp were two political signs planted in the grass, bright blue, advertising the campaign of some local politician. I not only noticed them but experienced a sudden chill because they read, in bold lettering, DUNCAN, DUNCAN; and what sort of sign it might be to see one's surname twice repeated at such a moment, whether I should have taken it for a lament, or as a marker pointing homeward, I could not, at the time, have been certain.

By the time you reach Rockwall, the skyline of downtown Dallas stands twenty-five miles distant like a collection of monuments against the flat horizon. For months I had envisioned myself stopping on the side of I-30 East to have a moment, standing in the median looking back on the city from the other side of Lake Ray Hubbard, traffic blowing past me. Behind me, facing east, would be a moving truck loaded with all my worldly goods. That moment would serve as the perfectly symmetrical bookend to my time there.

But that morning the skyline was obscured by mist, and by the time I climbed the long, low hill at Rockwall, the one that affords that view of shimmering skyscrapers—what had looked, to this boy from the country, like some great Emerald City of earthly delights and hope and Providence—only a dull white sky stretched to the horizon, as though I had only imagined the events of the last three years, or as if, while I slept, the city had packed itself up and stolen away in the night like a gypsy carnival.

II.

I **STOPPED IN NASHVILLE** late that night to add a quart of oil to my jeep. Heat radiated from the engine compartment like an oven and that old Mopar V8 smelled as if something might be permanently spent in the effort to get me home. *Just get me there*, I prayed. I'd spent the day driving in silence, watching road signs loom and then pass, ticking off the miles between the cities. Texarkana. Little Rock. Memphis. Nashville. Knoxville. Bristol. I had plenty to think about.

Sometime after midnight, I crossed the Virginia border and began to see snow lying on the fields, gleaming under lights in the distance like varnish on the landscape. Earlier, my father had offered to drive some distance south and meet me on the road to drive the last leg of my trip. Tired as I was, it had seemed an irrational offer, creating as many problems as it solved. I didn't know anything then about being a father. I later learned, hearing the story from my mother, that he had sat up waiting until I pulled in the driveway at three a.m. He had set a kitchen timer to remind himself to pray every thirty minutes for my safe return.

I would be remiss to allow the reader to conclude that from this point on I went on with my life and never looked back, learning the lessons that were rightfully due me and becoming as mature as I ought to have been by then. In truth, the first thing that happened, within a week of arriving home, was that I became profoundly depressed. Limping home from Texas again only reminded of my failure to establish a life for myself ten years before, and brought back a vivid sense of the shame I'd felt on my return, zombie-like, from the psychiatric ward.

I tried to pick up where I'd left off with my Virginia friends, but they would find me staring into my beer or gazing into some far corner of the restaurant. I looked at other women across crowded bars and tried to imagine starting over. I looked at pictures of my ex and began to wonder, remorsefully, if our problems had really been so bad as the situation in which I now found myself.

I only texted her at first, and then we began talking on the phone, sometimes for three or more hours a night, and like some marital peace accord, those conversations went on for a month. I even flew back to Dallas and stayed with her one weekend, and I even thought, for several hours after I arrived, that it might really work out after all.

The psychology of our relationship was exactly like a vase that had been shattered and glued back together—well enough that it still held water, but it could never be the same. The fracture lines were there, in her face and in mine. A palpable sense of sweetness and self-surrender was gone. Our bodies were the same, but our consciences were seared. We had been children before, now we were like veterans who had each killed their share of men in a war. If that war was to be over, certain terms would have to be met. We each had a list, and neither list quite matched, nor would they ever.

We did touristy things in the city as though we had no idea how to conduct ourselves. And in truth we didn't. We wandered the gardens at the Dallas Zoo and stared at the primates, at turtles and flamingos and creeping things of the sort Adam had named once on his God-ordained quest for a mate. Appropriately, an orangutan, incensed by the mere sight of me, loped to the glass and executed, with a resounding gong, a perfect jump kick to my face.

That night, over dinner, the conversation finally turned frank, and words were said that I have not the heart to enumerate, ruining yet another delicious meal at our favorite Tex-Mex restaurant. It may seem callous, but I never could help staring at those plates of carne asada and thinking of how much money I had just paid for cuisine I no longer had the heart to taste.

The morning I left, she kissed me the way women kiss you when they're trying not to ruin their lipstick. Eyes open and lips firm. She turned in the doorway. We were only waiting for my worker's comp payment to come through, she said.

That's right, I affirmed joylessly.

She drove to work and I stuffed my pack and walked downtown with it hunched over my back like Pilgrim under the burden of Sin, like some scene of John Bunyan's from Vanity Fair. I stopped to have one last burger and Guinness at the Angry Dog, and then I walked to the monorail station and rode to the airport in silence and began to regret that I had ever wavered.

I'D BEEN HOME NEARLY a month when I recorded the following entry in my journal:

"The night my ex-fiancé told me she might be pregnant, I had a dream. I dreamed I was afloat on some large inland lake. I was in the water but I had a small raft or some piece of flotsam, a yard-arm or chest, the kind of wreckage one drapes oneself over after the classic disaster at sea. I looked up, and ranks of dark waves rolled toward me, a sudden squall.

I was driven to the shore, swimming in the current as one struggles to reach the bank of a fast-moving river. The shore was muddy and reeded and wild, like the banks of a wilderness lake in Alaska, the surrounding forest impenetrable for all its beauty.

I looked to another shore, some miles distant, a hopeless swim against the waves, which blew across the lake like a storm of divine appointment. I had a sense that I had blown off-course, that I had been headed toward that opposite side, that there were people there I wanted to be with, warm fires and conversation. But the wood came down to the lake in a swamp of reeds and fallen logs, and there would be no walking the shore."

IT WAS NOT FOR vindictive or petty reasons that she waited twenty-four hours to take the test. As long as she waited, a certain world remained at least possible. I understand now that it was her last hope of a claim upon me, her last hope of a future we might share, her last hope that she might, as Tamar did by the tokens Judah left behind, possess me at last—if by nothing more tenuous than a claim laid against what remained of my honor.

It would have worked, too.

In my mind, the future divided into two very different courses. Down one, I was a father, leading a little blonde-haired boy out into the woods, hiking and camping, teaching him the names of trees and birds and squatting with him to look at bugs, searching his face by the campfire for features that were mine and features that were hers and others that only we together could have made.

That Sunday, after sitting through church and trying very hard to concentrate on the pastor's sermon, I hiked up to McAfee's Knob to burn some nervous energy. When I got to the top, I sat the rocky ledge overlooking the Catawba Valley. Facing me, five miles distant, like a geological book end, were the ragged cliffs of Tinker Mountain, separated in that ancient upheaval from the very rocks on which I sat. Across the valley to my left ran North Mountain, a long, rolling ridge that led all the way back to the gap where Highway 311 passes by Cove Mountain. If you could see it through the trees behind you, Cove Mountain would hardly appear significant. At just the right time of day you might be able to make out a piece of daylight between the incisor of Dragon's Tooth and the surrounding trees. But that day I could hardly enjoy the view.

I dug my cell phone out of my pack. I'd been waiting all day for her to call or text, ever since that morning when I'd specifically asked her to go ahead and buy a home test kit. I'd been out of range of the cell towers while I climbed the mountain. On the summit though, there is always signal, and glancing at my phone, I saw that I had a message waiting. I went to it and it said, "Ian, test negative."

I looked out over Catawba, at the quilt-work fields and pastures, the undulating green mantles of the nearby mountains, and faint blue ranges in the distance, and I felt, instead of relief, that vision of my future son fading, because it had, after all, turned out to be only the most ephemeral of things: a dream—beautiful without regard for practicality—and I felt it die within me, quietly and without protest. I had created nothing for all my striving. For all the love I gave her, it would not live on. No living person would ever embody the cold and rushing creek we waded in Arkansas, the roses I brought her at work, or the meals we'd eaten in her kitchen on barstools by the stove, eagerly recounting what had happened that day; no one would memorialize the nights we'd carried our dinner to the bedroom to watch movies, balancing wine glasses and champagne bottles and chocolates and cartons of raspberries on the wobbly end tables, sometimes knocking them over, lamps tumbling, light bulbs exploding, flashing in the room like lightning and wine bleeding into carpet fibers we would scrub again and again in vain.

I was free to move on now, free to hike down the mountain and forget the things men try all their lives to remember. On the face of things, my ex-fiancé had turned out to not be pregnant, and I doubt anyone I passed on the trail that day could have understood why that disappointed me.

☀ ☀ ☀

DRIFTS, GRANULAR, DIRTY, and melting, still lay high in the mountains when I began hiking that spring. I sank nearly to my hips when I tried to walk across them. I scooped up snowballs and packed them, numbing my hands. I sat in the sun on the summit of Tinker Cliffs, drinking snow melt I'd collected from a drip among the rocks, and gazing down the valley toward the hazy silhouette of Cove Mountain.

Already, I could scarcely see the gray fabric panels of my cubicle, but I remembered them well enough that, alone in those woods, I had spread my arms wide and shouted, like an escaped lunatic, "I'M FREE!"

And I was. I was free to linger on those summits, one after another, finding what I hoped was a silence and solitude that would eventually coalesce into healing. It might surprise some that I never listened to earphones or carried books. I came for what the mountain had to give me. On some of my worst days I carried scraps of paper on which my mother had carefully written out verses of scripture, a habit which irritated and humbled me for reasons I could not have explained. A few I committed to memory, repeating the verse as I hiked, and unfolding the scrap of paper on the summit to read:

"For thus says the One who is high and lifted up, who inhabits eternity, whose name is Holy: 'I dwell in the high and holy place, and also with him who is of a contrite and lowly spirit, to revive the spirit of the lowly, and to revive the heart of the contrite.'"

I became a haunt of wilderness places. One day in particular, I remember hiking up to Dragon's Tooth and coming down again and staring at my jeep in the gravel parking lot for a minute before I turned around and headed back up the mountain. There was no reason why I couldn't. No one was waiting for me at home. I was free. But freedom, in its absolute form, can be terrible.

※ ※ ※

I WALKED OUT TO my jeep with a razorblade and scraped off my Texas registration and inspection stickers and removed the license tags that had been a declaration of my independence and a symbol of my new-found freedom.

THE LONE STAR STATE, they read.

I had been dreading this little ceremony, screwing on Virginia tags with some strange new number, going to the DMV and handing the clerk my Texas driver's license, the smiling thumbnail picture of me, the patchy goatee I'd grown while writing my first novel. The clerk held a punch over the top corner of the license and squeezed it, little pieces of laminated chad falling to the floor. She handed it back to me.

VOID, the punch read.

She told me to stand against a blue screen and look at the camera, but the camera was mounted too low and there was no changing it so I had to lower myself to get in the frame, my quads tremoring, much like squatting over a third-world toilet.

You're not allowed to smile, she said.

THE HEARING WITH THE judge came via teleconference and there was a lot of state your full name for the record and blah blah blah and in the end the only thing I took away from the experience was that the attorneys I was up against—the ones representing my employer—possessed a mastery of the law and domination of the courtroom that could have only been more obvious if I'd heard the sound of them scuffling with my state-appointed attorneys and giving them wedgies while they pleaded for mercy.

My attorneys had made some small misstep the other side was quick to exploit. Something had been filed incorrectly or some report was missing or some further medical examination would be necessary and the bottom line was the whole thing would be delayed again for several months. It was a brilliant strategy, really. Here I was, trying to assault the bastion of corporate America, and all the other side had to do was play the role of an insurgency until I became demoralized and gave up.

Thankfully, I still had Cove Mountain. I expunged my anger on that trail as though it were something in my bloodstream that could be metabolized. I went to the mountain with no intention but to lose myself, to be enveloped by wilderness or as near-wilderness as I could find. I met thru-hikers on their way from Georgia to Maine and joked, self-effacingly, that I was an unemployed, unpublished, disabled novelist. And then I would laugh. I had an easy manner with total strangers, but consciously avoided many of the friends I'd known for years, dreading the all-too-legitimate questions they might ask about what I was doing and where I was working (or not working) and what exactly I was doing with my time. My father more or less cornered me with several pointed questions to that effect one day, riding in his truck, and I had the temerity to tell him, offhandedly, that I was "waiting on God to show up in my life."

That my parents continued to shelter, feed, and encourage this prodigal should have served, had I the eyes to see it, as sufficient incarnation of the mercy of God. But I did not see it. All I knew was that reality was an inscrutable and implacable bitch, and the further I drove out of town on my hikes, the further into those woods I roamed, and the more miles I put between myself and civilization, the better I felt.

I poured myself into writing with the same strenuous abandon. The timelines I drew on yellow legal pads even resembled mountains: action rising to a climax and then falling away on the other side of the summit in the story's denouement. My first project was an unfinished novella I'd had time to ponder in my cubicle in Dallas while I had stared out the window and waited to be fired. I found it humbling and difficult at first, writing in my parents' house, but I worked out a system of laying the segments of my story in a linear progression around the circumference of my mother's mahogany dining room table, then mapping out the story on a single sheet of paper to see the big picture. I would walk around the table to "see" the scenes of the story playing out, then I'd return to that single sheet of paper to see it all at once, to keep it organized, and to ensure solidarity of theme.

I felt it went very well. Once the novella was finished, I printed a copy and gave it to a neighbor of my parents' who'd taught poetry at Roanoke College and studied under Annie Dillard at nearby Hollins University. If she was impressed, I hoped she might be willing to write me a letter of recommendation to an MFA program.

Almost as soon as I'd made the decision—if you could call it that—to move back to Virginia, I'd been working to recast my failure as a strategic retreat. I was returning home to regroup, save money, and work on applications to graduate school. It was my go-to story when I ran into people I knew; an almost entirely optimistic outlook on my life that managed to ignore nearly all the weighty forces conspiring, like a trash compactor, to press in on every side until I was utterly reduced.

The next piece of writing I turned to was my long-postponed guilty pleasure, the zombie novel I'd begun two years before, the one about the outbreak of a killer fungus based on real-life *Cordyceps militaris*. Here was the literary equivalent of the wilderness I'd been searching for: a 100,000 word, four-hundred-plus page project I could lose myself in for months on end. I threw myself into it obsessively, some days working at it as many as fourteen hours, completing as many as seventeen pages. I began with the forty-page seed (or perhaps I should say *germ*) of a novel from my old apartment in Dallas, and within six or seven weeks I had three hundred pages and seventy-five thousand words, easily three quarters of a draft.

I was reluctantly aware that I was steaming ahead in reckless optimism, investing myself in the very thing that had not worked before. I wrote in my journal that "the very definition of insanity is continuing to do the same things that have not worked in the past, over and over. This could also serve as a working definition of the life of the unpublished, aspiring fiction writer. I'm writing because it's what I do and I love it. I'm writing like it's going to save my life. I'm writing for my future, for the hope of independence and marriage and love. I write onward, into the insane impossible, until the world accepts my fictions and renders them real in print."

※ ※ ※

I FINISHED THE FIRST draft of *Cordyceps* on a hot afternoon in June, nearly six weeks later. I printed it out and patted the pages together and gazed at it from across the room with satisfaction: nearly an entire ream of paper. Apart from this memoir, no one who reads that story of a world infested with a strange and terrifying plague could possibly imagine what a Narnia it became for me in the process of writing it, what a delicious escape it provided, spending nearly all my waking moments immersed in it, working on it, thinking about it, from my morning coffee until late at night, when I would realize I was no longer forming sentences but only staring at my laptop screen.

That afternoon, I took my parents' golden retriever, Dudley, on a walk across the farm, stopping on a hilltop where I often picked blackberries along an overgrown fencerow. The field was freshly mowed, the air nearly one-hundred degrees, the sky blue, only cotton-ball clouds floating by. I ran a victory lap around the field in a fit of exuberance, shouting and holding my arms over my head like the first runner to break the tape at the end of the Boston Marathon. Dudley watched from the shade.

I had about ten dollars that I'd borrowed from my father, which I spent on four pints of Guinness. I went to a cookout that night with friends—purely happenstance that the party coincided with the completion of my book. Only one of those friends even knew that I'd been writing a novel, and he only casually acknowledged the accomplishment when I told him. I drank my pints of

Guinness and spent much of the night in my own thoughts while the conversation without me revolved around matters of the sort my friends were primarily concerned with: engagements and weddings and all their serendipitous courtships and marriages.

I drove home depressed.

"Ultimately," I wrote in my journal, "a writer writes for himself, lonely as that sounds, and satisfaction and success are things he defines for himself."

"I SEE YOU IN the future," the fortune teller in the cartoon says, "making the same mistakes you made in the past." Had I been one to ponder such wisdom, I might have realized the only thing I was demonstrating, by my concerted efforts to get my life together, was that I was precisely the kind of person who will never be able to get his life together. Something fundamental had been misplaced. I had botched the foundation of the house, but attempted to lay out the upper stories anyway.

Never mind starting over; never mind examining, as the makers of a failed flying machine might, one's underlying assumptions about flight, gravity, and the nature of reality. I intended to leapfrog over the lost years and resume the race at the same spot my peers had reached by years of faithful plodding. What I needed, I thought, was quick success with my new novel, a girlfriend, and a clear path forward in my career.

A month after finishing my novel, I began dating a waitress that slipped me her phone number on a piece of receipt paper while I was out having lunch with my mom. I was somewhat loosened up and smiley after the beer I'd just had, and I was surprised to hear myself flirting with her, considering, between her visits to the table, how crazy I was to think I could pull off a dating relationship, broke, unpublished, and unemployed. The whole encounter shocked me so much I went out to Catawba that afternoon and hiked a mountain in the rain.

It turned out, fortuitously enough, that my new girlfriend had recently bought a house, and she had a lawn that needed mowing and projects that needed doing, and her father owned rental properties that needed painting and remodeling, and before long we could joke about the little economy we had established, whereby I worked for her father and her father paid me and then I spent the money on his daughter.

I knew from the beginning that it wouldn't last. The truth is, I knew before the main course of sushi rolls made it to the table on our first date that I had no real business being with her. But I was tired of being alone, and I had reached a point—a very jaded and dangerously dishonest point—where I had enough life experience to know better and just enough weariness of soul to not give a damn. After two months of dating, I referred to her in my journal as "a very pleasant distraction." I was living out another Hemingway story, whereupon a man and a woman play games saying the things they know the other wants to hear, and make, by their mutual cooperation, something pleasant that does not quite equivocate love.

I should make clear there was nothing wrong with her—at least not the way things were wrong with me. She was the prettiest and most responsible woman I'd ever dated. She was a hard worker, a fantastic cook, and religious, too—and far more earnest in her faith than I was in mine. She had a fat little Buddha on a shelf above her toilet and a pan of charcoal under a tightly stoppered sink in her bathroom because a Feng Shui expert had warned her that particular vanity cabinet was, according to the ancient Chinese art, located in the same place as her romance, and of course, she didn't want the romance in her life to, well, go down the drain.

I felt a twinge of deep and repressed guilt when she showed me that. I felt like a con man being shown the treasure I intended to plunder. I must have known, even then, that I would leave her eventually, and I must have known, too, that she deserved someone better than me—a sincere pagan, at the very least, instead of a sham and a prodigal.

EIGHT MONTHS AFTER FILING for worker's compensation, it was becoming obvious that I was no closer to a settlement than when I'd started. The latest ignominy of the whole affair was that my own attorney wouldn't even return my phone calls. I don't even remember how it all ended, to be honest with you. At the time, I even despaired of writing about it in my journal. I vaguely remember my case running into more delays and my attorneys demonstrating further incompetence as I encountered, at every turn, a stultifying apathy emanating from the bureaucracy, until I finally realized it would be preferable just to move on—even injured—and simply get on with my life.

"One feels the indifference of the system," I wrote, "and one's insignificance to it, like so much shit being squeezed through some great and terrible digestion."

The construction work I was doing quickly made the symptoms of my nerve entrapment worse, until the months of rest I'd had seemed to be undone and the pain was as bad as it had been when I left my job in the cubicle. I tried to explain to my girlfriend that the work I was doing wasn't sustainable, that it wouldn't last, but I wasn't sure she knew what I meant. One problem was, I never looked like the kind of guy that should have carpal tunnel. For entire years of my life I had to laugh and politely answer strangers in public who wanted to know where I played football. Carpal tunnel? Isn't that something old secretaries and maybe the school librarian gets?

Paint jobs were the worst. By the end of the day, due to numbness in my fingers and the fatigue of atrophied muscles in my hand, I'd be executing a follow-through stroke with the paint brush and accidentally sling it across the room. That happened quite a bit. One night, I had to sign for a purchase at the cash register and found that I couldn't pick up the ink pen—had to make several attempts, as though I was wearing mittens. I often slept poorly because of the throbbing in my upper arm, and perhaps because of a growing sense of disquiet in my mind. The pain and discomfort were making me irritable. Alone, there were several choice phrases I would frequently mutter under my breath, including "Shoot me in the face," and "I'm seriously going to shoot myself." Back when I'd lived in Dallas, I'd told my friends I'd shoot myself if I ever had to move back to "Blownoke," as we called it, and now here I was, testing that very theory. Here I was, doing it all again, making all the same mistakes. I already knew how this story would end. Why, oh why, was I in bondage to disaster?

CIVILIZATION PERSISTS, I IMAGINE, largely because the steady gaze of a good woman rightfully goads a man to go make something of himself. Being in a relationship forced me to articulate some sort of plan for my life, and by that fall I had begun spending my mornings studying for the Graduate Record Exam, brushing up on algebraic equations I'd never wanted to resurrect, and memorizing one hundred vocabulary words, delicious words like "impecunious" and "salacious." Sometimes I would carry flash cards with me while I hiked, holding them at the twelve o' clock position on the steering wheel while I drove, the way I'd seen my dad hold his Greek and Hebrew vocabulary cards while driving on LBJ Freeway when I was a kid.

For several weeks, I studied and worked problems, filling legal pads with numerical scrawl. I reminded myself how to do long division. I studied sample essays and took practice tests in a cold sweat, grading myself and attempting to predict my score using the provided charts and tables. I went over my flash cards before I went to sleep at night and had dreams about solving for x.

I passed the GRE with verbal scores in the 99th percentile (let's not talk about the math) and compiled a list of ten MFA programs out of the top twenty in the nation, all full-ride scholarships, including UT Austin, UVA, Notre Dame, Cornell, Michigan, St. Louis, Florida, Vanderbilt, Minnesota, and Indiana University.

Statistically, the odds of being accepted at any one of these schools was dauntingly slim. The Michener Center at UT Austin, for example, accepted, at that time, less than one half of one percent of applicants. The fiction program at the University of Virginia, though only three hours from my hometown, received an average 630 applications each year and accepted only seven.

Essentially I was walking into a casino and piling all my chips on one slot of the roulette wheel. But never mind that; I had plenty of busy work to take my mind off probability, and even worse, I had the audacity to once again invoke Providence in my journal, falling back on the old proverb, "The lot is cast into the lap, but the decision is the Lord's."

What I could not deduce, from the lack of lightning striking me at that point, was this: uncoupled from a life of obedience and actual submission to God, a belief in Providence becomes a kind of charmed superstition, a strange form of externalized pride. I am the exception to the rule, it declares. I will be the one to crawl through shit and come out smelling like roses because once upon a time, when I was four years old, I did God the service of believing in him, and now it's only fair to expect him to return the favor.

I spent the next two months working on my applications, slowly checking off boxes on the spreadsheets I'd created to keep track of every component: thirty letters of recommendation, thirty college transcripts, multiple online applications—often separately to the university and the graduate school for each program, submission fees, purpose statements, writing samples, and deadlines rapidly approaching. By the time I finished I was having obsessive dreams about filling out those tiny little boxes with dates and personal information, always the anxiety of making even the smallest mistake, providing the selection committee with the reason they needed to narrow an exhausting supply of candidates.

Nearly as soon as all ten applications were submitted, I became preoccupied with the outcome, with finding out exactly what I had or had not accomplished. In my journal at the time I cringed to consider the sting of ten simultaneous rejections, "but consider the possibility, the slim, wonderful possibility of even one acceptance: finally, some validation of all my writing efforts, some tiny encouragement. What vindication that would be!"

Now that the applications were complete, I had a sense of loss much the same as I did upon finishing a novel; the process had, I realized, served as a welcome distraction, and I even admitted "my need for some engrossing project or object of obsession, some outlet for those fearful energies which threaten to undo me completely in boredom."

One thing was certain: something big was coming. Either progress in my career of the sort I'd longed for, or a tsunami of rejection so big it might crush me altogether.

WITHOUT DISTRACTION, my mind began to churn on the problems I was having with my girlfriend. The longer we dated, the more obvious it had become that we really had little in common besides compatible body parts, which, it must be admitted, do go a long way in cementing a bond—as intended by God—and therein lies the problem.

She wasn't a reader, for one thing. I began to suspect this one day when she turned to me on the couch and looked me in the eye, her lovely face only inches from mine, and told me, "I'm not a reader."

To her credit, she was enthusiastic about my ambitions the same way she would have supported any of my career goals. She liked having a good man in her life; maybe she even loved me.

I could have been an aspiring astronaut or figure skater and it wouldn't have mattered. But she did not, I must have known even then, believe in my writing with the kind of love or fanaticism necessary to weather the rejections I feared were on their way.

Every serious writer knows about sucking up rejection. Jack London famously had a stack of them rumored to be five feet tall. To a writer, even hundreds of rejections don't mean the same thing they would to a sane person. Six hundred rejections, for instance, don't mean you're a deluded fool who'd better find something else to do with your life; it only means it's going to be all the more epic when you finally succeed; it means that one day, when the historical society is giving guided tours of the hovel you once lived in, the guide will pause, ironically, in a room literally *wallpapered* in your rejection slips. *But nothing could deter him from success.* That kind of thing.

But how can you really expect a non-literary type to go along for that ride? When you first meet a girl and tell her you've just finished a novel and that several New York agents are looking at it, success seems very possible and even imminent.

"How much of an advance do you think you'll get?" she asks.

Six months later, your heartbreaking work of staggering genius (as Dave Eggers calls it) has been rejected a dozen or so times and you're still living with your parents. Just imagine how that looks to a normal person.

In retrospect, I can see how miserable I was, how acceptance into an MFA program had already become, in my mind, the rescue I needed from the latest inextricable mess I'd made of my life. I had a lie going on both sides of town, and I was pushing both sides of that lie beyond any credibility I had remaining. On one side of town I was a respectful son who came home every night—albeit late sometimes—and most certainly was *not* sleeping with his girlfriend. On the other side of the city, I was a passionate lover who waited until his girlfriend fell asleep, or at least long enough afterwards, before rising and putting on his clothes, that he gave her no reason to suspect that his heart and affections lay elsewhere.

The truth was, not even I believed my lies anymore, and I despised myself for it—or maybe I only knew I *ought* to despise myself for it, and therein glimpsed the infinite regress of my sin. It slipped out in conversation once—quite accidentally—that I didn't think we had a future together. We'd been discussing *what ifs*: What if I was accepted to a graduate program in Texas or Michigan or Missouri—then what? The truth was revealed by way of omission. I carefully skirted the offer, even hypothetically, of her going with me to grad school. She would have, she told me, through tears. She would have gone with me to the ends of the earth, and the truth of the matter was, I was only sleeping with her.

An unforeseen consequence of holding out hope for my own future—a future without my girlfriend—was that I became troubled by that very topic. As she would later put it during one of our last fights, "My wiener got a conscience."

Of course, it wasn't right, to begin with; and suddenly, for some reason all too convenient, I could no longer ignore that fact as I had been doing quite successfully and without interruption for the past five months. Certainly, there had been moments, late at night, driving across town, when my convictions or perhaps even the Holy Spirit himself had begun to confront me, but then there was the welcome oblivion of sleep, and the next morning there would be a text message saying she was thinking of me, and then, of course, hope springs eternal, beautiful and irrational, and somehow it will all work out—somehow, surely, grace will abound. No merely theological belief can supplant human love. A genuine love for God—for the person of Jesus himself—could safeguard you against that, but no mere principle, no mere list of oughts and ought-nots stands a chance against passion. It was never meant to.

Now the dichotomous worlds I had attempted to maintain began to slowly, tortuously separate, like a paramecium dividing or surgical tape being pulled from the skin; and my heretofore easy traffic between those worlds began to seem like the perfidy that it actually was.

"What if you were to get pregnant?" I argued, not unreasonably, but stupidly still.

"I wouldn't *have* it," she assured me. She might consider carrying it to term, she said, and putting it up for adoption—sometimes you could get as much as $10,000 for doing that.

Things fell apart from there. I would later have time to wonder how a relationship that began out of such pleasant and beautiful impulses could very nearly have led me straight into complicity in murder or the abandonment of my own flesh and blood. A pit opened up before me and I glimpsed a little bit of my own hell. She came back at me with the admission that she didn't really believe my nerve-entrapment syndromes were keeping me from gainful employment: if I was able-bodied enough to hike mountains and type emails and write short stories, I should be able to work a job. She suggested I become a postal delivery man or a bank teller.

I told her I'd get back to her in a couple days.

THE FIRST TWO REJECTIONS came hard and fast, like a double tap. I had spent the first three weeks of February in a state of quiet agony, second-guessing my entire life and compulsively checking my email to the point that I actually began to have an endocrine reaction every time my phone vibrated, my breath halted and my lungs burning, my heart beating in the back of my throat and the taste of pennies in my mouth while a progress wheel spun and I stared intently at my inbox, waiting for new messages to download.

The first arrived while I was standing in line to buy a pound of whole bean coffee at Starbucks. I saw that the message was from UT Austin—my first choice among all the programs I'd applied to—but I didn't let myself look at it until I'd bought the coffee and driven home, ground the beans, poured the grinds into the cone filter, and set the pot to brewing, talking myself down from hope all the while, like a hostage negotiator, calmly and logically, assuring myself that if I had really been so fortunate as to be one of the six applicants accepted out of a *thousand*, they wouldn't be sending an email, they'd be calling to personally congratulate me—they'd be landing on my lawn with a helicopter, knocking on my door with bunches of balloons and a giant cardboard check like Publishers Clearinghouse.

When I opened it, the email directed me to log into the University of Texas website with my temporary student ID and password, whereupon I scrolled down to see a little pale blue box, and inside it a few short sentences, the gist of which was "Based on the recommendation of the Creative Writing Department your application for admission has been denied." Which, I wrote in my journal that night, was "slightly less meaningful than GAME OVER flashing on the screen of an arcade game. At least in that case you know you should have shot more aliens."

The second rejection was much the same, from the University of Washington at St. Louis. Those first two rejections were, in some ways, the most discouraging. They were the ones that burst the fragile bubble of hope. It was depressingly easy, now, to imagine eight more rejections following close behind.

"I hate the way ambition ruins so much enjoyment of the present," I journalled, "always the striving for something better, the superiority of the dream, and its inevitable standard for evaluating one's present circumstances: this is not the life I want, you think, and only a small step further for Pride to wink and assure you this is not the life you *deserve*, either."

I began to imagine that I could distinguish between an insignificant vibration of my phone, say for junk mail, and the profound throb of an arriving rejection. Times the WIFI connection was slow, I might stare at the progress wheel for entire minutes before I swore and set the phone down, paced for a few minutes, and tried again. I became irritable, sensitive, and petty. In an entry entitled "Damned and Broiling," I bemoaned the fact that there was a nice-looking brunette sitting in the coffee shop not ten feet from me with "perfectly tanned legs; legs for which I could not even presently afford to buy the moisturizer necessary to maintain that bewitching sheen."

One of my childhood friends emailed me out of the blue, eager to share with me the details of his blessed life—listed in bullet points, no less: his lovely bride of eight years, his three wonderful children, and the job he was enjoying every minute of. And how was I doing?

"I have floundered into such a vexed state personally," I wrote in my journal, "that redemption cannot come fast enough. I find myself, like the victim of some vaudeville thriller, bound hand and foot and riding a conveyor slowly toward a giant sawmill blade, calling out for some providential rescue, but knowing all the while that the scenario is of my own construction and that, very likely, I will be reduced to quarter-inch strips before help arrives."

I had a particular table at the local coffee shop that I felt I had to have in order to get anything done. It was located along the wall by what appeared to have been an old doorway, now bricked-up and dressed out with fluted posts and a peaked cap pediment in the Greek Revival style. It seemed the sort of charmed doorway that Gandalf himself might have approach with staff extended, muttering some elven riddle.

If that table were occupied, I would take another nearby, ready to transfer to it the moment it was abandoned. The light there was good, too, coming down from a skylight. It was a slightly larger table than the others, the perfect size to arrange my laptop, journal, and a mug of Russian tea, the bag left to steep until it acquired deep tannins and notes of leather.

Even with the ideal set-up I was depressed. Once, on the way to the coffee shop, I turned the car around and drove home, dreading the sort of morose navel-gazing I was bound to record in my journal that day. "I don't know why I came here," I wrote the first week of March. "To sip lukewarm tea and people watch, I guess. I'm tired of introspection; I'm tired of sounding like Eeyore in this journal."

I needed another project. I found it in a parody of *The Road*, which I entitled *The Comet and the Cockroach*, featuring a cockroach and a stink bug in place of Cormac McCarthy's father and son traveling through a post-apocalyptic wasteland. "I don't think

I have ever laughed so much writing a story before," I wrote. "Maybe I'm cracking up..."

I received five rejections while writing that story, hearing back from two more MFA programs and several short story submissions to literary journals. I was trying to be brave and professional about it, writing, "There are far too many rejections in this business to mourn every single one... No, you'd never make it, thinking like that. You have to take it the way a boxer takes a blow." But in truth I swung like a pendulum from the hilarity of my fictional world to some of the lowest lows I'd ever experienced.

I would drink, and when I did, a zoetrope of scenes from happier times with my ex-fiancé would flicker across my mind's eye. "Don't ever do this to yourself, if you can help it," I wrote. It sounded like something I'd told the clerk at a drugstore checkout once, stopping on the way to my girlfriend's house to buy condoms and a five-pound bag of ice. I had to pay with loose change because it was all I had left. "Don't ever let your life come to this," I told him. My conscience was seared but not completely; I had no wedding band and knew I was casting myself as a particularly poor example. Poor kid must have wondered about my intentions for that bag of ice.

About that time, I wrote in my journal that I had simply grown accustomed to almost daily thoughts of suicide. "This will seem a shocking admission to anyone who has not lived with depression on a daily basis, who cannot possibly understand how quotidian such thoughts can become, the way soldiers in a warzone become familiar with death... Anyone but a psychiatrist could eventually come to understand that this is not an emergency to be dealt with by drugs and hospitalization, but a deep and irreconcilable trait that one must learn to live with, the way amputees must live with the ghosts of their missing limbs." But not to worry, I added, almost as a postscript, if I were that kind of man I would have done it already. "If God wants me dead, he'll have to do it himself."

* * *

REJECTIONS FIVE AND SIX came through the U.S. mail in the form of printed letters. The first, from the University of Michigan, had been folded into thirds before the ink dried, blotting itself in stigmatic repetition across the body of the letter—probably not a good portent, I thought, for being accepted into one of the most prestigious MFA programs in the country.

"Dear Applicant," the letter began ambiguously, "This has been a record year for our program—both in terms of the number and quality of applicants..." Always that crucial cushioning sentence to soften the apology to come: "We regret to inform you," or "report to you," as though all these letters were drafted by devotees of an honor culture, but Michigan's rejection terminology was truly unique—in keeping with the high standing of the institution, I suppose. After some further prevarication regarding the limited number of slots, only the best prepared candidates accepted, and so forth, it read: "We regret to inform you that in this highly competitive pool of candidates, your application was not successful."

I was impressed with the sense that I had missed some drama in miniature, some distant competition to which I had sent an unlikely representative: a pinewood derby, or a horse race on which I had improvidently wagered a large sum. But even more strangely, the obfuscation of this phraseology made me feel that some deeply personal part of my very being had been sent out into the world only to fail: "We regret to inform you that the spermatozoon of your application was not quite vigorous enough to implant itself in the egg of the MFA program and has subsequently died in the vaginal acidity of the Department of Admissions."

The second letter was from the University of Indiana in Bloomington, and although it had not, apparently been sent in as much of a hurry, I only needed to scan halfway through the blocked out paragraphs to find the words: "I apologize to inform you..." before tossing it over my shoulder into the backseat of my jeep, pretending that it mattered but little to me, as though I would not later retrieve it and smooth it out and read it several times, examining the weight of the paper, the quality of the letterhead, the offhanded professionalism of my rejecter's signature.

※ ※ ※

ONE OF THE HARDEST things for writers to accept about the process of sending out submissions is that very seldom do rejections include any feedback or offer any reason for the rejection, and therefore present very little opportunity for learning. I couldn't say, "Well, the University of Washington thought I used italics indulgently," or "The University of Austin was unimpressed with my alma mater."

The only time during that bleak month of rejection that I received a personal note, it was from the Missouri Review, whose editors (or perhaps only interns), scribbled on the side of the rejection slip: "We really enjoyed the style and subtle humor of this piece and hope to see more of your work soon." My enthusiasm over that little note was tempered by a friend who opined, eloquently, that accepting a compliment imbedded in a rejection was "like licking the icing off a shit cake."

I began to construct purely hypothetical narratives—some of them pathetic, some of them self-righteous—in a vain attempt to placate my ego. I began to imagine my academic credentials must not have been impressive enough, or more cynically, that perhaps even religious discrimination might have played a role.

"All of us here at Cornell got a good laugh out of your application," I imagined a more honest rejection letter might read, "what with you—an unpublished Christian college graduate from backwater Appalachia, (hold on, my sides are hurting) HOME-SCHOOLED, no less—thought a couple of short stories would get you into the hallowed, ivy-covered halls of our institution. But best of luck with your nascent career as a humorist."

I decided that the Legend of the Undiscovered Writer was a myth, that the cream most certainly does not always rise to the top, and that there was, in fact, a substitute for good writing, and that it was popularity and prestige.

I imagined the insurmountable slush pile at every literary magazine, the fantasy that some open-minded editor would actually invest countless hours in the objective consideration of every submission, even a writer such as myself, with no credentials, no publishing credits, and no prior success whatsoever.

Despite the legends of famous writers toiling in obscurity and leaving behind their undiscovered masterworks, I feared that selection committees would only be reasonable to expect a future author to bear at least the tiniest indication of promise: they would teach at a college or university and have some small but respectable publishing credit to their name, or perhaps they would have won a literary contest or earned an honorable mention.

I had none of those things. Of course, I also had to admit, without having been a fly on the wall of those selection committees, that I would never know for certain that they hadn't read my stories carefully and with an open mind, thinking about them for several days while they ate and showered and put on wool turtlenecks and drove to the university in their late model Volvo wagons; perhaps they had even brewed coffee and gathered in the faculty lounge with my manuscript lying on the table before them, and only then, after much sharing and discussion and gesturing with their hands, decided that my writing hopelessly sucked.

"Suffice it to say," I wrote in my journal, "I am disappointed."

✳ ✳ ✳

I FOUND THE NOVELLA I'd recently submitted to a literary magazine returned all the way from Alaska only two weeks after I'd sent it—hard to believe the post could even reach Alaska and return that fast. They must have switched from dog sleds to snow machines that year. I had enclosed an SASE with plenty of postage, half-hoping I might be so lucky as to tempt some editorial feedback, even the disgusted kind: perhaps a red line angrily drawn through the very first sentence and some dismissive comment in the margins. But my pristine manuscript, laser-printed on twenty-pound, ninety-six brightness paper had only been folded in half and stuffed in the mailer—no dog-eared edges or even wrinkled margins to indicate the friendly squeeze of a human thumb and forefinger. On the cardstock rejection slip, a woman in her early twenties had written in that bulbous, friendly, internly hand, both the title of my novella and "many thanks," which, in the context of having apparently rejected my story as quickly as possible, seemed almost sarcastic. But this was only a typical rejection, even old-fashioned in these days of online submission managers, immaterial emails ghosting through the ether, mouse-click rejections at the ease of a twitching index finger, or more recently, the "auto rejection" received in your inbox seconds after clicking send: "Dear Author, Unfortunately, your submission does not meet our present needs. (But in the off-chance that we actually are interested, we'll let you know.)"

At this point, only two MFA programs remained, and in my memory the applications I'd sent them were beginning to seem as preposterous and cute as the Snoopy-themed birthday card I'd sent to President Ronald Reagan as a child. Was I expecting Air Force One to come rotoring over the treetops and land on the front lawn? At least the Reagan administration, God bless them, had the decency to send me a magazine splashed with full color photographs of the President going about his daily routine in the White House. Notre Dame had only sent an email notification announcing, ominously, "A decision has been made." Once I logged in to see my rejection letter, I could print it out at my own expense if I wished. Minnesota did the same, using the exact same web-based application management software.

I drove to the coffee shop and wrote in my journal about the financial problems plaguing my parents in the wake of the recession. It appeared they might be on the verge of losing everything. My mother had taken a minimum wage job at JoAnn Fabrics and had recently chipped a tooth eating almonds and had to have the jagged remains of the tooth ground smooth until she could afford to have it capped. My father's farm was for sale for a fraction of what it had been worth only months before. Just as he had reached retirement age, the world's economy had died beneath him, like a racehorse collapsing on the final straightaway of the Kentucky Derby. There would be no coming back from this one, I knew. No going back to restore, in short order, the wealth built fastidiously over three generations. In the space of a single year, my parents had gone from driving new cars and managing investments to being turned away by lending managers and having to borrow twenty dollars here and there to buy groceries.

"Meanwhile," I recorded in my journal, "their thirty-two year-old boomerang son masturbates nostalgically to the most tasteful free samples of online porn he can find, showers, and limps his high-mileage Jeep Cherokee with minor body damage down to the local Starbucks-alternative café, where he drinks the black tea of the day and writes pensively in his journal, crossing out "stock phrases" and replacing them with their more literary equivalents, describing, with resolute dignity, his latest rejection while he listens to Pandora internet radio in his earbuds via his iPhone and nurses his delusion of becoming a moderately successful mid-list author, which, it is plain for anyone but him to see, is merely a cover for a discontented, downwardly-mobile lifestyle consisting of a series of ten-month stints at various jobs for which he is never suited, denied graduate school applications, expired health insurance coverage, and an alleged nerve-entrapment syndrome; but—and this is what makes it all worthwhile for him, you see—he has recently finished editing his collection of unpublished short stories."

*　*　*

I DID NOT BOUNCE when I hit bottom. In an entry titled "Hope Fizzles Out," I wrote "If this were a baseball game, the bleachers would already be clearing out... I don't know which is more ridiculous, giving up before the last rejection letter arrives or holding out hope until that very moment."

It was the last day of March. Only the University of Florida and the University of Virginia remained. From what I'd learned about the administration of MFA programs, Florida would have likely notified their accepted candidates more than a month ago, giving them time to weigh their options (presumably between the multiple offers they had received) and reach a decision, and March 31st was rumored to be the last day UVA would contact any of its applicants. In some circumstances, of course, the program's first choice might have declined an offer in favor of another school, and there was always the possibility they might still be contacting the next candidate on the list... perhaps the very last name at the very last hour... Hope can be cruel.

"It is now 4:26 p.m.," I wrote, "and more obvious than ever that such a call is not imminent."

I drove home from the coffee shop and opened the mailbox, only to have a rejection letter from the University of Florida spring at me like Nately's whore. (I was reading Joseph Heller's *Catch-22* at the time.) Later that evening, I was on the internet looking at a picture of the flotsam skeleton of a pelican, all the plastic garbage the bird had swallowed readily visible through the slats of its exposed ribs, when an email popped up from a creative writing professor at UVA, kindly letting me know that I had, regrettably, not been chosen for admission. It was depressing, let me tell you, just to think of those poor pelicans scooping up big beakfuls of assorted product packaging, and all that ocean garbage swirling out there in gyres the size of Texas. Also, I'd just been rejected by ten graduate schools.

In my journal I launched into a rambling historical explanation of why MFA programs were currently harder than ever to get into; why acceptance rates at top programs were typically under 2% (Harvard has a 6% acceptance rate, by way of comparison) and how the best time to become a novelist had really been in the 1980's, and how I'd essentially just bought ten lottery tickets, or, given the statistics for UVA's program, engaged in a game of musical chairs with 800 competitors and only ten seats.

I imagined starting over, going back to get an undergraduate degree in English—what I should have done in the first place. "I suppose I'll sit in my parent's house and consider various alternatives left to me, such as growing out my hair a foot long, or shaving it off altogether, or maybe getting a couple tattoos, or other deep thoughts that occur to one drifting out on the brackish riptide of frustration toward the horizon of unimpeded lunacy."

THE COMING WEEKS BROUGHT me one good reason, however temporary, to go on living: Heath Coles was flying up from Dallas for a week-long visit, and fully expected to be provided a tour of my favorite wilderness locales, and—more importantly for an outdoor type granted a reprieve from urban life—to hike and camp as much as humanly possible.

I began planning immediately, unfolding long maps of the local Appalachian Trail and plotting waypoints for the ideal forty-mile, three-day excursion. It came down to one of two options. The first was a section hike in Catawba known as the Triple Crown, putting together three of my favorite summits into an epic one-way trek: Dragon's Tooth, McAfee's Knob, and Tinker Cliffs—all unforgettable experiences for a first-timer. The alternative route was through the Mt. Rogers National Recreation Area, near-ly three hours away, which included the Grayson Highlands, a Narnia-like wilderness populated by half-wild ponies of the kind that seem to have a magical penchant for emerging from the mist with shafts of sunlight radiating from their manes. But that hike, unfortunately, came with the complication of arranging pick-ups and drop-offs from one end of the route to the other, details that were simple enough to arrange, even in those days before Uber—unless you happened to be quite as nearly flat broke as I was.

I decided to make the most of my resources close to home, that is to say, my mother, who would happily drop us off at the trailhead and pick us up wherever we decided to stop. Further preparations included the purchase of a four-pack of Guinness Draught—the pint cans with nitrogen widgets rattling in their bot-toms, which were as close as I could approximate the pints Heath and I had often raised at The Angry Dog back in Deep Ellum. I packed those beers out approximately six miles to a point we'd reach from the opposite direction at the end of our first day's hike, and stashed them under a slab in a cold-running creek that comes down from Tinker Mountain. I grinned all the way back to the car, imagining the look on my friend's face.

EVEN THAT FIRST NIGHT, I sensed an unexpected spiritu-al significance to our conversation. We sat on the back deck of my parents' house, smoking Padron Anniversarios and sipping cognac Heath had brought from Texas. I spoke honestly about the bitter disappointments, bouts with depression, and break-ups I'd had that year—more honestly than I ever would have over the phone. And it was good. I had nearly forgotten my friend's wit, his raucous laughter and hard-edged political commentary. It was hard to believe, but in only a single year of isolation, I had nearly forgotten the joy of iron sharpening iron. It meant the world to me that he had come.

We warmed up with a day trip to Rockbridge County to see the Devil's Marbleyard in the James River Face Wilderness, getting our fill of bouldering, stopping to marvel over stunted bonsai pines that survived, seemingly without soil, between the rocks, and exploring deep crevasses where the air was cool and dank and bore a scent as ancient as the earth itself.

Back in Salem, we geared up, stuffing our packs with sleeping bags, titanium cookware, pouches of freeze-dried food, water purifiers, Sven saws, flasks of whiskey, guns, knives, and various other provisions more than sufficient to establish a homestead in the wilderness, let alone sustain us on a three-day foray into the woods. I can't speak for Heath's pack, but mine weighted fifty pounds.

The next morning, we drove my jeep out I-81 to Daleville, windows rolled down and Cake blasting from the speakers: "Nugget" and "War Pigs," both of us belting out the lyrics, gesticulating violently, and practically dancing in our seats—nearly forgetting my mother riding in the backseat, who, to the credit of her maternal generosity and forbearance, only brushed away the hair blowing in her face and looked on as though she were an anthropologist observing some curious rite of masculine friendship.

We got to the trailhead parking lot, shouldered our unbelievably heavy packs, waived good-bye to my mom, and exchanged grins of the this-is-going-to-suck variety, the type which strong young men, for some reason, find so exhilarating in the presence of other strong young men.

We struggled up the side of the first hill in early spring heat, Heath panting up a switchback thirty yards behind me, while I secretly grinned with pleasure that I'd devised a physical challenge that could take the breath of a Rambudo black belt candidate.

I pushed us hard the rest of the day along the winding ridge of Tinker Mountain, stopping only to look out over the wind-driven surface, far below, of Carvin's Cove Reservoir. By dusk we'd made twelve miles, only a mile from the summit of Tinker Cliffs, our goal for that first night. It had been an interminable climb upward, and we were both tomato faced. I had been cruelly teasing Heath's subconscious thirst for several miles, asking, at various intervals, what he thought the fair market value of a cold beer would be, just about then. He had only huffed sweat off the end of his nose and proposed a sum approximating the national debt.

We dropped our packs within sight of the creek, dug out our pump-action water purifiers, and decided to tank up for the night, since it would be our last water opportunity before pushing for the summit. I tried to string Heath along for a couple minutes with some nonsense about finding just the right spot to filter water, while he passed me glances like he thought I might have had a heat stroke or otherwise lost my mind, until at last I stepped down to the bank, heaved aside a big slab of stone, and astonished him by reaching into the water and lifting out—like some quintessential beer commercial—four pints perfectly chilled by a clear running stream.

We made the cliffs by sunset. We dropped our packs, kicked off our boots, swung our legs over the edge and sat looking out over the lights already twinkling on the floor of the Catawba Valley. I distributed the beer, and we cracked them open and I took a picture of Heath raising his first pint gallantly in honor of the Salmon King. There, against the backdrop of a red horizon, I pointed out our next two summits: the smoky blue outline of McAfee's Knob six miles away, and in a distance paler still, the strange-shaped ridge of Cove Mountain, where Dragon's Tooth waited as it had, I suppose, for a thousand years.

WE SAT UP THAT first night around a campfire not far from the cliff's edge, building up a ring of stones to shield the flames from a persistent wind. The next morning, we slept in. I was in a single-man tent and Heath had brought an orange bivy sack that looked more like something for biohazard containment than a comfortable sleeping arrangement. In the morning, I made coffee in the little titanium French press I carried and we had a leisurely breakfast of reconstituted eggs and oatmeal.

We had no intention of trying to set any mileage records. Those trails were so familiar to me it seemed we were only hanging out in my backyard, but something was different. Something nearly intangible, as though breathing that mountaintop air was serving to clear my head. And that sweeter air seemed to provide, not just clarity in general, but a perception of unseen realities, and it happened by such slow degrees that it came upon me quite unexpectedly. Perhaps it had begun when, on that first long hill, we had decided to name our packs, realizing at once the intimate relationship we would have with those burdens before the adventure was over. Heath named his "Ruby" from the Cake rendition of the old Waylon Jennings song, and I dubbed mine "Sin" from the famous burden of John Bunyan's Pilgrim, an uncomfortably honest admission of the true weight I carried over those hills, and for the next two days I would have the increasing sense that the trail and even the act of backpacking itself had become a sort of living metaphor—not as though it reminded me of *The Pilgrim's Progress*, but as though I were *in* the story myself.

That morning, oddly, my conscience was troubled. We had spoken over the fire, as men sometimes will when wreathed in the darkness that surrounds that single bright point in the night, of our lost loves and heartbreaks, and it had become apparent to me, in the course of our conversation, that during my last year in Dallas I had been so absorbed with my own relationship problems I hadn't been much of a friend to Heath when he had needed one.

Perhaps it would be more honest to say that my conscience, long-suppressed, had been reawakened. I thought to apologize to him for an old sleight—on our last camping trip, in Alaska, Joel and I had disparaged him for his meticulous stowage of gear each time we broke camp. It was nothing, really. Or perhaps I was beginning to see that it *was* something, that so many of the behaviors I'd dismissed as "mistakes" and "bad choices" or excused as trivial were actually deep offenses to someone—or worse yet, a capital Someone—and more accurately labeled by that ancient and ugly sounding three-letter term from the bible.

I had learned in seminary that the wilderness often serves as a motif for spiritual confrontation, a place where the devil meets and challenges his adversaries brazenly, a place where God performs his most astounding miracles, where mighty men of old fell upon beasts in desperate combat and ravens brought food to prophets and seemingly chance meetings led to salvation—in short, where battles are waged; and it began to occur to me, with every stride along the trail to McAfee's, that those bare and unpeopled woods where I had long made my own wilderness wandering might be the very place where I would have no choice but to reckon at last with God and the devil or the emissaries either might send.

The trail to McAfee's wound up the steeply pitched backside of Catawba Mountain, past monolithic gray rocks covered in lichens, and through tunnels of rhododendron that could not have been more beautiful if they had been planted in a botanical garden. Here, the trail was so old and the plants so long grown around it, only the white blazes that marked the Appalachian Trail gave it any manmade sense, and it seemed, rather, that the trail itself was a thing intended by the Creator, a thing grown there, as those God-tread pathways in Eden must have seemed long ago.

We stood on the summit at McAfee's and I took pictures of Heath posing on that rocky outcropping cantilevered out over the blue valley below, one of the most iconic images of the Appalachian Trail, and frequent choice of photographers for good reason.

We had lunch on the rocks, but pestering black flies drove us from the summit before we'd quite planned, and as it was still early in the afternoon, we decided to press on and make our camp on the trail between McAfee's and Dragon's Tooth, wherever nightfall found us.

We made camp that second night by the trail that runs along the rolling spine of Catawba Mountain, still a good ten miles from Dragon's Tooth. We were footsore and weary, but not so weary that I wasn't tempted to hike back down to the road and hitch a ride to the store to buy more beer. I left Heath to build the fire.

A local man on his way home from work picked me up at the McAfee's trailhead parking lot. The car reeked of cigarettes and his daughter rode in a child seat in the back. Probably because I looked and smelled the part, he took me for a thru-hiker on my way from Georgia to Maine, and I didn't correct him as I should have, stealing the honor of those that make that great trek, mostly because it easier and less embarrassing than admitting I was only a local boy on a jaunt, taking advantage of him to make a beer run, not some footsore traveler worthy of congratulations or a free ride to the store for supplies.

We made small talk, and I continued to pretend that I didn't know the area—lies which came all too easily for someone that had spent too much of his life trying to bend reality to his wishes. He graciously offered to wait while I went into the store, and even when I emerged with nothing more critical to survival than two six-packs of beer he drove me back to the parking lot where he'd found me, making his day that much longer, postponing his and his daughter's dinner, and even kindly refusing one of the beers I offered him before I climbed out of the car. I thanked him and told him he'd made me a very popular man on the trail, as though an entire shelter full of hikers would be blessed by his Trail Magic.

Walking back into those dark woods, I kept replaying in my mind how quick he'd been to refuse even a single beer, how he'd held up his palm against it—there was a history there, I decided, a guarded weakness that my careless and false interaction with him might have even disturbed. It was only another of my many sins and I pushed it out of my mind. What seemed like two miles into the darkness, I approached a glowing orb of firelight among the trees, my shoulders aching and a six-pack swinging from each hand. Heath grinned and swore.

We made merry before a roaring fire, and that night I pitched my tent across a bed of moss and slept as well as I ever have in my life.

✴ ✴ ✴

I AWOKE TO FIND several missed phone calls and text messages from my mother, sounding frantic, her voice breaking up in a message I could barely make out: something about a storm, a severe storm warning for that night. Naturally, she thought we should come off the trail instead of camping on Dragon's Tooth, as we'd planned. I had to admit, chilling on top of a three-thousand-foot mountain during a major electrical storm was, to put it in the parlance of our hiking guru and Alaskan friend, Joel, "highly inadvisable." Heath and I talked it over, but rather than cutting our hike short, we decided to extend it even further, ("Further Up and Further In!" from *The Chronicles of Narnia* had become our rallying cry) beyond the summit at Dragon's Tooth, five more miles over some of the most difficult terrain in the Appalachians, to a remote shelter called Pickle Branch—all before the storm broke at nightfall.

We spent the day hiking south—against traffic for those making the traditional northbound thru-hike, so we had plenty of opportunities to warn other hikers of the impending storm, advising them to get to a shelter or even spend the night at the Four Pines Hostel rather than risking it out in the open, where even a single falling limb could crash through a tent and prove fatal.

It was a gorgeous, cloudless day, and nearly everyone we spoke to had no idea a storm was in the forecast, much less a severe one. They frowned and looked at their trail maps. Again, I was struck by a strange, somehow prophetic feeling, rife with metaphors, that we were out on the trail warning other wayfarers of an approaching storm that only we two witnesses seemed to know about. Everything we did and said—even the copperhead we saw camouflaged in leaves beside the trail—seemed to be imbued with secondary, spiritual significance, as though an unseen realm, normally hidden, had begun to make itself known.

We made the summit of Cove Mountain two hours before dark. It had been a brutal climb with full packs. South-bounders have often told me Cove Mountain is the most technical terrain they've seen since Mt. Katahdin in Maine. It was an easier climb for me, buoyed by an almost masochistic delight in the exertion, as well as the joy of introducing Heath to my favorite mountain, practically my home away from home that first year back from Dallas.

We wrestled our packs to the ground, suddenly lightened, and climbed to the uppermost precipice of the dragon's tooth, enjoying a panoramic view, clear for nearly fifty miles up and down the Catawba valley. We looked down on hawks cruising unseen currents. From that summit were visible most of the pale blue hills we had toiled up and down the past three days—thirty-eight miles of trail.

I told Heath this was the spot, more than any other, where I had worked out my salvation with fear and trembling, where I had argued with God, where I had prayed and where I had once dared God to take my life with a thunderbolt, finally running down the mountain while lightning exploded around me like mortars in a warzone.

There, on that uppermost rock that knifes into the sky, with our feet dangling over the edge, Heath gripped my shoulder and prayed, what seemed, as my eyes flooded, the most otherworldly prayer anyone had ever offered for me. I couldn't help but imagine afterwards that Heath's prayer had *done* something, that it had made some real change in the world, though what it entailed I had no idea.

It didn't seem, at first, any more ominous than a typical afternoon storm. We could see it approaching from the west, a bank of thunderheads towering into the upper atmosphere over Potts Mountain, and darkening the horizon toward the border with West Virginia. Perhaps because of the endorphins released in our climb, or because that spectacular view was the reward for all our miles, we lingered there too long, and it was not until we noticed lightning flickering along the top of Sinking Creek Mountain that we realized it was well past time to get going. We shouldered our packs and set out down the backside of Cove Mountain, the wind picking up and the light quickly fading, the sunset soon blotted out by the storm, and I began, for the first time that day, to consider that I might have made an error in judgment.

A KIND OF DARKNESS more sinister than nightfall overtook us as we picked our way along the rocky downward spine of the dragon, deep leaves and angular rocks making it difficult to hike quickly. We stopped only to strap on our headlamps after Heath nearly sprained an ankle. The better part of me was concerned for everything that could go wrong—and go wrong very fast—but the worst part of me felt the same, almost perverse enthusiasm for disaster I'd felt as a child when the Texas sky turned black and tornado warnings ran in a red ticker across the bottom of the television screen. It was all still an adventure at that point, and had I been truthful I might have told you that adventure was what I wanted out of life—perhaps more than anything.

But something about that night began to unnerve me. Perhaps it was the abject darkness visible on the horizon beyond the trees, or the forest canopy already swaying overhead, or the trail that led ever downward, much further than I remembered, as though it had been extended and repeated, mile after mile, by some cruel magic.

Many times, sitting atop Dragon's Tooth, I had been the first to laugh when day hikers went running down the trail upon feeling the first drop of rain. I wasn't afraid of being caught out in a storm, but I was growing to fear this one. The very air was charged, the barometric pressure plummeting. We were too far down the trail to turn back and retrace our steps over the mountain to the parking lot that was only 2.5 miles from the summit. I had treated this like any ordinary storm, but it was not. It was somehow evil, and its slow build-up, the amount of time it blew and threatened before the rain came seemed to indicate, on a subconscious level, its massive scope.

It was nearly nine o' clock by the time we reached the half-mile spur trail to the Pickle Branch shelter, and lightning had begun to flicker soundlessly through the trees. I swept my flashlight beam over the shelter when we came to it, essentially a three-sided sleeping platform with a roof, and when the light fell across the plank floor it illuminated what appeared to be a prostrate figure in brilliant white robes, but it was only a thru-hiker sleeping in a white bivy.

We bypassed the shelter and went down to the creek to get water. The sleeping hiker was yet another let-down; it meant we might not be able to enjoy a leisurely campfire, eating our dinners, laughing loudly as we always did, and winding down with cognac and cigars. We found a ring of stones several hundred feet from the shelter, built a small fire, boiled water for our freeze-dried meals, and with a cheerful bit of ceremony, I brought out the two remaining glass bottles of beer I had carried an ungodly distance just for that moment.

We sat on the ground by the fire and our spirits revived with the food and beer, but by the time we finished eating, raindrops had begun to spatter us, and gathering up our gear and hefting our packs, we had to walk back to the shelter in a full downpour.

We sat against the back wall watching the storm through flashes of lightning, sipping cognac from our flasks and making conversation with the Thru, whose trail name was "Tree Frog." (Heath and I had been giving our trail names as "Frisbee" and "Platitudes," respectively, names we would later change to "Dragonsbane" and "The Magician's Nephew.") Tree Frog told us how he had started the trail in Georgia with the enthusiastic support of his wife and kids, fulfilling his life-long dream of hiking the entire AT. We discussed the terrain that lay ahead, resupply opportunities, and scenic spots not to miss.

I sat up watching the storm after Heath and Tree Frog turned out their headlamps and zipped themselves into their bags, Heath on my left and Tree Frog on my right. I had sipped enough cognac that I should have been relaxed and carefree; instead, as I watched the rain—torrential, and without end—I became increasingly uneasy. Something was not right. Something about our situation was not right. I went over the thru-hiker's story in my mind, considering the seeming improbability of a loving wife with children encouraging her husband to embark on a six-month hike from Georgia to Maine. But that, for many, is how strong they find the call of the woods, as John Muir said, "The woods are calling and I must go," and I had no reason to suspect the man to be disingenuous except for the inexplicable and increasing sense of danger I felt.

I turned my attention to the storm itself. I scooted forward to the open side of the shelter where I could sit with my back against a post and scan the surrounding ground in flashes of lightning. I had a Glock .45 in a Ziploc bag beside me, the bag unsealed, but no round in the chamber. I began to think, and I remembered that less than five miles from that shelter, up Sinking Creek Valley, two college students out camping had been murdered in their tent, killed in such a horrifying way, apparently, that the police had withheld all details. The killer had never been apprehended, but I had seen notices posted at the trailheads announcing rewards for information leading to an arrest.

Why did I have this irrepressible sense of vulnerability? Was it paranoia? Was I cracking up? Was there some serial killer haunting this valley, waiting for his next opportunity to stalk hikers in a remote campground? Might it even be the stranger beside me, posing as a thru-hiker, waiting in that shelter the way a spider waits in a web?

The longer I watched the storm, the more convinced I became that the danger was out there, in the darkness. I was not afraid—strange, but I was as calm and resolute as I have ever been in my life. I determined to keep watch over Heath and Tree frog. Perhaps that was what I was supposed to do; the greater purpose in my uneasiness.

I sat up all night.

The storm itself was monstrous and fascinating. I did not know then how many hundreds it had already killed, that it was the *storm itself* that must have given me the foreboding sense of a killer's presence. Sheets of rain swept the night like a monsoon, like the tropical downpours I had seen in Hawaii, only this one lasted four or five hours. Several times I scooted to the edge of the platform, lay on my side, and urinated over the edge, the rain so loud my own water could hardly be heard spattering below. I kept my hand on the grip of my .45 and scanned the surrounding woods, sector by sector, one sector per lightning flash. The shelter was surrounded by a clearing perhaps forty feet across, and I felt confident I could rack the Glock's slide and hit anything that tried to cross that distance. My eyes had long since begun to play tricks on me, whether from exhaustion or the lack of visual stimulus in the dark, I don't know, but I expected it: little flashes of red dots like glowing eyes at the tree line. I even had some fun with it because it seemed my brain could make anything I imagined appear from the darkness: gnomes playing football, whatever I wanted.

When I noticed something suspicious, some dark silhouette or shape, I'd watch it until the next flash of lightning, then move on to the next candidate. I passed some of the time praying for Heath and even Tree Frog, and just in case I should fall asleep, I held a penny in my mouth as a "stim," an old trick of soldiers on the night watch. A couple times I woke when the penny fell to my lap from my open mouth.

I had my hand on the Glock—inside the Ziploc bag because of the drifting mist, but I began to have the sense that whatever was out there was not the kind of enemy that bore any concern for such weapons. I can't explain to you how I knew that something was out there in the rain, watching us—or even if I really did know—and I can't say anything to convince you that it was even a warranted suspicion. I have since talked to several other men who have had similar experiences in the night, a sensation, as the witches in *Macbeth* put it, that "something wicked this way comes."

At one point, I became certain there was a man-sized silhouette standing at the edge of our camp, though it did not move and I did not trust my mind to remember whether or not a stump of some kind had been there before. I confronted it with prayer, though what right I thought I had to venture, weapon drawn, into that realm, I could not have told you then, nor could I now.

THE FOREST GRADUALLY BRIGHTENED from black to blue gray with the breaking dawn. The world was still there. Tree Frog got up groggily and packed his gear and we spoke in hushed voices about hiking, necessary equipment, and my own ambition to hike the entire trail one day. I made some excuse about my nerve pain keeping me awake during the night. He strapped on his pack, smiled, shook my hand, and headed up the trail, and that, oddly enough, is when strange things began to happen.

It has been nearly nine years now, and I have written in my journals about every other aspect of the storm and the things that happened afterward, except for the hours that passed that morning, when suddenly, I could barely form sentences, could not conceive how to pack up my mess kit, as though it were a baffling cognitive puzzle, and I even made Heath put my pistol in his pack for fear of what might be happening to me.

I managed to remember my way down the mountain, though I had to stop and rest and at those points I would weep for reasons I could not rationally explain, although it seemed as if the full burden of my sin had descended upon me and neither pride nor self-love could shield me from it any longer. I remember lying back in the passenger seat of my jeep, watching Heath drive, watching him wipe away tears from his eyes while I babbled incoherently, like a man in a trance, telling him I had to get someplace where the water was pure.

I remember thinking, at the time, that I must have been poisoned by water I had filtered from the creek near the shelter, or that I had suffered a heat stroke, or worse still, that my deepest fears about my own mental instability had come to revisit me, and that I was having another nervous breakdown. But I have never been able to believe that, partly because of what came after, and partly because the nature of it was so completely different. To this day, I can only describe it as being struck by confusion. One minute I was myself, albeit exhausted from keeping watch all night, and five minutes later I was rendered incapable of tying my bootlaces. Perhaps my past renders me an unreliable source of information. I'm sure you could find a psychologist or two that would agree with that assessment. A pastor I once confided in told me my experience had "no spiritual weight," which, I understand, makes sense within the limited purview of a strict systematic theology, but makes no sense at all of what happened next.

Heath got me back to the house, where I tried to explain to my mother that I thought I'd suffered a heat stroke and further begged her not to call and have me committed. She assured me she had no desire to do any such thing. I was deathly afraid of going to the hospital, for fear of what might happen to me there. I took a shower, shaved, and asked Heath to read the Psalms to me while I laid in bed and wept into a pillow. Whenever I closed my eyes I saw serpents writhing. I was afraid to be alone, afraid of the dark. That night I asked Heath to bring in cushions so he could sleep on the floor of my room.

I woke during the night and said, loudly, "WE ARE UN-AFRAID," as though some deadly enemy were standing in the very room. My consciousness seemed brackish, a mixture both rational and irrational, sane and insane; some of the things I said were intelligible, while others were delirious.

From the floor came Heath's irritated voice, telling me to go back to sleep.

I slept again and I dreamed that my soul was moving through a series of chambers, like passing through the rooms of a house, and the last and furthest remove was some boundary that could be crossed but once before all was lost. I woke in the night and quoted scripture aloud. I was not afraid to die, I was afraid to be *lost*.

The dread that came over me was as close an experience as I have ever had of the pure fear of God. I knew, all pretenses stripped away, that I was a phony, that I had played games with religion, that I had exploited my theological knowledge in order to pass for a much more authentic believer than I ever had been.

I knew where my soul rightfully belonged were I to die that night. I woke again and went into the small bathroom adjacent to my room, knelt on the cold tile floor, and said "I submit, I submit, I submit." It was, after all, the authority of God, not the knowledge of him or his existence that I had so long resisted; it was his right to command my life, to deny me my pleasures, to demand my faithfulness—those were the aspects of his Lordship I had long resented.

Heath woke up. In the darkness of the room, he shone his flashlight beam on me, where I sat on the floor, leaning against a dresser, as physically wrecked as if I had just run a marathon.

"Now I will live to serve the Lord," I said.

THE NEXT DAY I refused to leave my room. I told Heath I needed to sequester myself for three days, a number which seemed to irritate him but seemed to me a reasonable timeframe for resurrection. Several times a day, Heath brought me plates of food from the kitchen, and if I was hungry between meals I had a jar of almond butter I ate from with a spoon. I lay flat on my back on the floor quite a bit, at perfect peace now, drifting in and out of sleep, and for those three days my nerve pain disappeared entirely.

Late that second afternoon, I was kneeling on the floor reading my bible by a west-facing window. The skies had been swept clear in the aftermath of the storm, the wind still blowing as though the front had created a vacuum in passing.

The sunlight lay bright across the onionskin pages of my bible. As I was reading, I noticed the light fade, as though a cloud had passed over the sun, but when I looked up, I saw, out the window, not so much as the wisp of a cloud, but the entire, round sun hanging in the bare sky, and that orb a weak and sickly red, like a dying star. While I was staring at it, the light came back full strength, and I looked away, blinking and confounded.

Again the light faded, and again I looked back, just as shocked to see for a second time, the same wan sun, perfectly round and uneclipsed, like a blood moon at midday. Again, the light came back, and again I looked away. A third time the light faded, and I returned my gaze skyward, awestruck by the sight. The light came back again and I sat staring at my bible, where it lay open to the book of Joel: "your young men shall see visions," and several verses down, "And I will show wonders in the heavens ... The sun shall be turned to darkness and the moon to blood, before the great and awesome day of the LORD comes."

I sat in stunned contemplation of what I had just seen with my own eyes. The fact that I did not run from that room, shouting through the house, should only serve to reveal the strange state of my mind and soul that day. It was, after all, only one of the many strange things that happened, and in some ways, I suppose, it would prove to be the least incredible. I did casually ask Heath, when he brought up my dinner that evening, if, say, anything interesting had happened in the news that day, fully expecting him to excitedly recount an outcry in the streets, full panic, riots, looting, and social order on the verge of collapse.

He shrugged. The same storm system that had enveloped us on Cove Mountain had apparently spawned 360 tornadoes and was now being called a "super outbreak," leaving a trail of devastation all the way from Virginia to Alabama, and at least seventy-five people were believed to be dead (a toll later revised to 348). Nothing else. No one else had seen the sun darkened that day. And there one of the mysteries that would haunt me for the rest of my life actually began.

✳ *✳* *✳*

I WAS STRANGE AT FIRST, when Heath and I left the house that third day and ventured out into public. He insisted an outing would be good for me. I let him drive. My syntax was off, strangely formal—I remember eschewing conjunctions for the better part of the morning as though I had, in those three days, traveled back in time and lost the memory of modern speech altogether, or as though my mind had gone through a great and violent reset with the bible as the only language to restart it.

We ate lunch at a café in Floyd and went for an unhurried hike in the highlands above Rock Castle Gorge. My thoughts were admittedly strange, perhaps even borderline psychotic, depending on who you asked. I briefly wondered if I might be some sort of prophet, granted a vision for the End Times, or if perhaps Heath and I were the two witnesses mentioned in the Book of Revelation—he obviously the more reluctant of the two, but you had to admit the math was there.

With every passing hour the strangeness faded. That was all. I was the same, but I would never be the same. I drove Heath to the airport a couple days later and tried to explain, while we waited for his flight, what I thought had actually happened, what the meaning of it all had been, how we had—perhaps inadvertently—engaged in spiritual battle on that mountain, beginning with Heath's prayer on the summit, and how the Lord had used that experience or the storm itself to break me and draw me back into the faith I had, by all rights, abandoned. It wasn't clean, it wasn't verifiable, it wasn't the sort of conversion that would ever fit into any kind of recognizable category; but even then, surely, you had to admit something significant had happened.

Heath listened as kindly as I think any friend or brother could ever be expected to, though I'm not sure he would ever be able to believe it—not for years, anyway—and honestly I wouldn't blame him if he never does. Ten years have passed and we have yet to speak of it again. You wouldn't have understood it either, if you'd been there. It was only *my* soul that hung in the balance that night, only *my* spirit dangling on that precipice between worlds, only *my* mind nearly shattered in the process. God had shown up in my life, in thunder and fury, and when he did, he had come for *me*, for this one Prodigal, for this one Lost Sheep, and he had come in a way that no one else needed to comprehend.

I may never know exactly what happened the night of April 27th, 2011, on the back side of Cove Mountain. It took me a year to even attempt to write about it in my journal. "There is more in this world than meets the eye," I wrote, "but there is also always a deniability, always a bare natural explanation for what happens, always an alternative to belief, and no recourse to verify that experience—or even to maintain one's own confidence in it during the long, unremarkable months that follow. It might have only been a nervous breakdown. Exhaustion. Dehydration. Copper poisoning. Sleep deprivation. Or it might have been more."

I BEGAN MY LIFE AGAIN. For a while it seemed everything had changed, so much so that the very world appeared to me in a newer, cleaner light. I had the sensation of being reborn, and for a while I presumed that the world had been reborn along with me and that all my past troubles would fall away like a scab from a wound already mended beneath.

I was done with passivity and misery, with the victim mentality begun with my unfortunate decision to file for worker's compensation. While the total relief from nerve pain I experienced those three days didn't last, it gave me hope that perhaps some lifestyle change could be made, or that some chiropractic adjustment might help. It set my imagination to wondering if there might be some physiological explanation for it—perhaps sleeping on the ground? Some food I hadn't been eating? I decided to forgo the first of the surgeries that had been scheduled for that very next week, and it only seemed a kind of confirmation a few days later when the surgeon's office called to cancel the procedure themselves, on account of the surgeon's wife having a baby. I would go forward in faith, and in the strength the Lord provided, from then on.

I was a man again, and a man had to support himself. I gathered together a load of scrap copper from the old barn where I had stored it back in my construction days and drove it to the recycling center that offered the best price per pound. That was the first three-hundred dollars I made. I sold many of the guns I had collected over the years, thousands of dollar's worth by the time I was done. Connections I made with old friends in the process of selling those guns landed me a series of odd jobs later that summer trimming trees and remodeling kitchens. I used a good chunk of the money I raised to buy a plane ticket to Alaska, where I spent three weeks having adventures with my friend Joel and working a journeyman carpentry gig I found on Craigslist, which paid for all my expenses. When I flew into Anchorage, I had sixty dollars to my name, and when I arrived back in Virginia I had twenty dollars and a bag of candied salmon, but I had done something most people only daydream about.

I wasn't the most responsible person yet—probably I never will be—but I learned by that experience that I could change things about my life. I could make things happen, if I really wanted to. I was a man, after all. I brought that attitude into my writing career and paid a friend from church with graphic design know-how to create my first website, IanDuncanBooks.com, where I would blog and announce the release of my first self-published e-book on Amazon, a novella about a trio of unlikely treasure hunters titled *Mouribon Cave*.

I became more social. I even joined Facebook, something I'd proudly resisted for years. I tried dating again, although no miraculous changes seemed to have occurred in that department. Four months after I came down from the mountain, many of the things I'd tried had still not worked. My life had not been entirely revolutionized. But my heart had. That August, I wrote in my journal, "I have made approximately six dollars from my efforts at self-publishing, I have a negative balance in my checking account, and the woman I fell in love with wants to be friends and won't kiss me anymore. Yet I am not the same. It no longer matters, you see, whether I am successfully published, or whether I have money, or whether a woman loves me. I have Jesus, and my future is assured. Perhaps, for all my effort I will never have the life I wanted. I may never see someone reading one of my novels on an airplane. I may never comfortably live the writing life; I may never pose for author photos in black and white—unsmiling, of course—with deliberately wild hair or that three-quarter pose with dramatic facial lighting that says, smokily, 'I have a dark side just like my books.' And what difference will it make? My absence from publishing will not even reduce the stack of outmoded thrillers discarded from the public library twenty years from now, for some other author will have taken my place in the publisher's budget. All that matters is that I somehow join the work that God is doing in the world..."

That first week after Heath left, I had gone back out into the National Forest to do trail magic for the thru-hikers. I packed in backpacks full of fruit, cold bottles of Gatorade, and granola bars for the hikers I met. I now went by the trail name "The Magician's Nephew," and made a little fun out of pulling full-sized watermelons from my backpack while thru-hiker's mouths fell open. I stocked a cooler full of ice and orange juice on top of Dragon's Tooth one morning, climbed up to the top of the rocks, and watched while exhausted Thrus lifted the lid and seemed to think they were seeing a mirage. I interviewed other Thrus and asked them what meal they wanted most on the trail. They said a fresh-baked apple pie, and I made that happen, too, intercepting them at a shelter on the next mountain where they were waiting out a rainstorm. Some of them emailed me after they finished their hike and said stories about my trail magic had circulated all the way to Maine that year. It was some of the most fun I'd ever had.

I holed up in a shelter one night with a pair of retired missionaries, one of them a Vietnam veteran and the other a former firefighter, and they told me stories about the adventures they'd had once they'd surrendered their lives to God. I wondered why I hadn't been granted some epiphany or clarion call to a specific ministry. The Lord had obviously interrupted my life and brought me to repentance, but what specific task had I been saved to accomplish?

I NEEDED A JOB, I realized at last, though it required a certain humbling of my adventuresome spirit to admit. Many nights during that time, I played chess with a pharmacist who was, by God's providence, exactly the sort of cigar-smoking, wisecracking mentor I needed during that season of my life. He helpfully nudged me in the direction of gainful employment as one might nudge a fledgling bird toward flight.

I applied for jobs as a pool cleaner, valet, policeman, lumber stocker, skid-steer operator, admissions counselor, cashier, librarian, and manager of a horse barn. The economic recovery from the Great Recession was underway in many parts of the country, perhaps, but it was hard to prove in southwest Virginia at the time, where, for instance, nearly three thousand people had applied for a job when the new Lowe's Home Improvement Warehouse opened. I know because I was one of them, and I even interviewed for the job, but for some reason not even my four-year college degree could get me a job stacking two-by-fours.

I sometimes remembered, with almost bittersweet nostalgia, sitting in my cubicle in Dallas, staring at a stark white sheet of paper lit by that harsh fluorescence, on which was printed my salary agreement, the four-digit number in bold ink I could scarcely believe: $3,333.33 per month, and now, two years later, I was standing in a grocery store staring at an eight-dollar bag of cashews, trying very hard to remember how it was that I had ever been able to afford such extravagant luxuries.

All the jobs I applied to turned me down. I nearly took a job back in Dallas cleaning pools, and interviewed with the owner of the company via Skype, but it was against my better judgment, particularly considering the kind of gripping and repetitive movements it would involve, much like painting, to say nothing of the lack of health benefits. It was too late and I was too broke for another wild lark, another round of crazy risk-taking, another big gamble. I needed to avoid unnecessary risk and build carefully on any advantages that I had accumulated. I had learned a little bit about life that summer by playing chess.

"I have been too depressed and anxious to write stories," I confided to my journal. "I had to stop drinking coffee because in the silence of the house, day after day, I was literally pacing the floors and pulling at my beard. It has been a year to try a man's soul."

I sent out another ten agency queries for *Cordyceps*, and those came limping back, rejected. By then, my most promising novel had been rejected by twenty literary agents.

Occasionally I would get rejections from stories I had submitted so long before that I didn't even remember them. I no longer even bothered to keep track of my rejections. Once again, there seemed no way to move forward by writing. "I have been more broken," I wrote, "but I have never been more frustrated in my life."

A friend of mine at the time encouraged me to think more faithfully—even more imaginatively—about what God might be doing in my life. She said God never tore down merely to destroy, but in order that something new and better might be built in place of the ruins. I don't know where she got that kind of wisdom, but it got me thinking.

"Suppose everything happening to me now is my very salvation," I wrote. "Suppose I turned my imagination in his favor and assumed that this period of loneliness is only the journey toward the *right* woman, that my afflictions are keeping me from the *wrong* profession, that my unemployment is giving me critical time to pray and mediate, grow and heal, and to realize things about life. Perhaps in my thanklessness I have seen only what the gift is *not*."

By late September, I was down to one hundred and twenty dollars and all the over-priced clothes I'd bought at Nordstrom in Dallas had holes in them from moths and campfires. I didn't even wear my dress clothes to church anymore, since I knew I wouldn't be able to afford to have them dry-cleaned on the off-chance that I happened to land a job interview.

I went through seemingly interminable doldrums, days in which absolutely nothing happened. I kept to a routine of sorts, though admittedly there were minutes, and by their aggregate, hours unaccounted for that I spent staring at some object in the yard or standing at the sink trimming my beard with a kind of nervous compulsion because, quite simply, I did not know what to do.

I spent hours on end searching the internet for jobs, until my hand began to ache and I realized that if I couldn't navigate a website without pain, how could I really expect to perform the types of jobs I found there? I applied to several more anyway, a seasonal customer service job at an Orvis call center, a position at Appalachian Electric Power as someone who would answer questions about employee health benefits—ironic, since I hadn't enjoyed health benefits myself in nearly twenty months—and a job in the post office at Liberty University, along with two other administrative positions on campus. It had been an entire month since my last interview. I had a drywall finishing and ceramic tile job coming up at my uncle's house that would pay enough to get me through another month.

"Besides my cell phone bill and my car insurance," I wrote, "I spend my money only on food and gasoline. The gasoline takes me to the YMCA and over into Catawba, where I spend an admittedly inordinate amount of time hiking and generally escaping reality on the Appalachian Trail. The endorphins are my therapy; between the hikes and my frequent workouts I have been able to hold depression at bay. Plenty of days I have driven into Catawba with tears in my eyes and come back smiling and singing along with the radio. Thank God for Cove Mountain."

✳ ✳ ✳

THAT FALL I HIKED up to Dragon's Tooth two or even three times a week. "For a few weeks," I wrote, "the woods are suffused with yellow light, and all around are suspended dimensions of brilliant leaves like confetti stopped midair. In the silence of the forest it seems each leaf waits its own turn to release and rustle downward, some gliding like paper airplanes, others flashing like tossed coins or spinning a pirouette on stem's end. Fallen, they lie across the trail in all their glorious geometry: serrated maples, blood red; palmate poplars, bright as lacquered paint; and a distinct sense of privilege or ceremony to tread there, like walking on rose petals in the aisle of a church.

"From the summit I see the Catawba valley as though newly painted, and that by an artist of peculiar yet perfect impatience for the predominance of any one autumnal hue: across the valley are striations of red and rust, while closer by, an entire ridge is lit yellow, and the contrast of that line of poplars with the evergreens behind them is stark as gilded scrollwork. It is nearly enough just to be there atop that highest rock, looking out over the valley, nearly enough the way the ocean or the night sky is nearly enough, and I suppose that is why I linger there."

I got a lot of thinking done on top of Cove Mountain. When I was writing *Cordyceps* and ran into some plot problem I would hike there and lay on the uppermost rock, my boots and shirt off, baking in the heat like some pagan sacrifice draped across an uplifted altar.

One of the things I often wracked my brain about was finding a way forward in my writing career—the "career" that so far had made me about enough money for a one-time purchase of a decent roast beef sandwich. I began to realize that the traditional model of publishing I had pursued for so long, the world of literary agents and big publishing houses, seven-figure advances and the lottery dream of an unknown writer finally being discovered—even the dream of that outcome was quickly going the way of the Dodo. The advent of the e-book had made it seem as though, within a few years, print books would be as antiquated and outmoded as VHS tapes and landline telephones. Even since my return from Texas, e-books had begun outselling print books, up 300% in only two years. It was a revolutionary time. At the coffee shop where I went to write, I began to notice people reading on iPads and iPhones. Borders, the second largest brick-and-mortar bookseller in the United States, had just closed its doors forever. Even the big publishers, desperate to hold on to their preferred way of doing business, had done everything they could to suppress the sale of e-books, holding back the release of digital editions to tempt impatient readers to spend twenty-five or thirty dollars on a clothbound hardback wrapped in a glossy dust jacket.

All that was going away in a big hurry. The internet had changed the world irrevocably. Worldwide distribution was no longer an exclusive service; anyone with a modicum of intelligence could upload a manuscript to Amazon's Kindle Direct Publishing and launch their own e-book, keeping a whopping 70% of the list price for their royalties. Authors didn't have to wait around anymore, plaintively knocking on the hallowed (but tightly closed) doors of New York City's most exclusive publishing houses.

For the first time in over a year, I could see a way forward in my career. I didn't have to keep waiting for one of the gatekeepers to let me in. I came to reluctantly accept the dying of a certain kind of dream we authors have, and to realize that upheaval in the industry had made it, quite possibly, the worst time in history to be an unknown, unpublished writer hoping to sign with a reputable house and behold the glory of his debut novel festooning the shelves of an actual bookstore. Conversely, though, it was the best time in history to be a self-published author.

All my pent-up energies were soon directed into the entrepreneurial development of my own books as investment properties. Jared Hall, the same friend from church who built my blog (at the time a teenager on winter break from his junior year at

JMU) helped me design the cover for *Cordyceps*. Jared and his brother Justin and I met in a coffee shop in downtown Roanoke, and after much brainstorming realized it was impossible to portray the iconic image of a sprouted climber on an e-book cover the size of a thumbnail on Amazon's website. We could only hope to convey a title, color-scheme, and perhaps one symbol. We pulled up Amazon on our laptops and squinted our eyes and noted the dominant reds and yellows of many best-selling titles, beside which the covers of other books seemed to disappear. We borrowed the canary yellow hue of Jon Krakauer's *Three Cups of Deceit*, added a bold red biohazard symbol, and played around with fonts for the title until we settled on one called League Gothic. Then we added blood splatter. There. We'd just saved eleven-hundred dollars, according to a quote I'd been given by a graphic designer in Chicago.

I spent several weeks editing *Cordyceps*—endlessly, it seemed, until my throat was sore from reading it aloud and I was having dreams at night about sentence and paragraph structure. I had already edited the entire manuscript a year before, but I read through it at least five more times searching for typos, missing punctuation, unintended alliterations, echoes, repetitions, missing words, and unnecessary attributives, until I was confident it was as perfect as I could make it short of hiring a professional editor or having a nervous breakdown.

By January, we were ready to release it. After Jared patiently executed several last-minute changes to the arrangement of blood splatter on the cover and corrected a few Kindle formatting glitches, the e-book went live at 1:05 a.m. I had a celebratory toast of Jack Daniels, dancing around the room to "Dirty Harry" by the Gorillas, (played on my headphones for mom and dad's sake) marveling to think it had all started on a legal pad at my old apartment in Dallas—four very long years earlier.

"Will it sell?" I wondered in my journal. "At the moment I have 133 Facebook friends, 15 followers on Twitter, and about $300 cash to my name. Unless *Cordyceps* proves to be as contagious as its eponymous pathogen, it seems unlikely that more than a dozen copies will sell. The good news is I'm so broke there is a very low threshold for success."

※ ※ ※

FOUR DAYS LATER, I drove out to Cove Mountain with a grin on my face because *Cordyceps* had sold fifteen copies. Most days that next week, I awoke before dawn, practically tremoring with excitement to check my sales numbers to see how many copies had sold during the night, the same feeling I remembered having as a child on Christmas mornings. Early reviews were nothing less than enthusiastic. Old friends messaged me their congratulations; I heard from my old coworkers at the Baylor Tom Landry Fitness Center: Chris Brumley, who had pantomimed smoking pot when I first pitched him the idea of fungus growing from people's heads, and Michael Snyder, who had first showed me the BBC video of real-life Cordyceps.

Every day brought some new text or tweet from excited readers. I received my first piece of electronic fan mail: an email from a reader who had devoured the story in two days on his iPhone and absolutely loved it and wanted me to get started on the sequel—an idea that Joel and I had actually discussed in Alaska that summer.

Somewhere along the way I had actually forgotten that writing books, while intensely satisfying for the creative mind, was actually something we do for the sake of *readers*, the *real people* who would spend hours with our books in their hands, following every line with their eyes, enjoying the previously unimagined places the adventure takes them, even the physiological effect it has on them, reading late into the night, page after page. One reader told me it had literally made her heart pound; she seemed genuinely shocked to find the cliché had some basis in reality.

Every morning, my sixty-year-old mother (who had been a fan since I'd called her from Dallas to read her the first version of Trubilinski's press conference) would find me in the kitchen making coffee and ask, sometimes breathlessly, how many books had sold during the night. We called it "checking the numbers." Mom celebrated every single sale, sometimes dancing around the center island in her flannel pajamas.

"The launch of *Cordyceps* and its initial reception," I journalled, "is the most positive, most encouraging thing that has happened to me in what seems like a very long time. The future is wild, unpredictable, and, in a thrilling new way, unlimited."

A MONTH LATER, a wave of exhaustion not unlike postpartum depression washed over me. This has been the case in the aftermath of every book I've written, a certain deadly quietness that creeps in after the initial elation burns away, a silence that fearfully confirms that the world, after all, has not been changed by the finished work, as it often felt it would during the white-hot energy of its creation.

So, now what? I had been back from Texas for two years. I was thirty-three-years old and living with my parents. I was seriously in danger of becoming Ignatius Riley. In my desperation, I batted around many of the same ideas that had failed to work in the past. I considered trying to join the Army. I considered moving back to Texas, where, from what I had heard, good jobs were still easier to come by. I considered the fact that my jeep's transmission was more than likely poised to fall out somewhere in the mountains of Tennessee.

I found myself staring at the contents of my old room, the disorder I had been able to ignore in the bustle of the writing and editing and publishing process. Before me was "a still-life of unopened bills and bank statements, defunct typewriters, and winter-crazed stink bugs trundling around the shades of burned out lamps. Two years! I look in the mirror and I see a hardened, bearded face that would have been as strange to me two years ago as the face of a castaway."

I had no way of knowing, then, that my novel would ever sell more than fifty-three copies in a month, or that what I had already accomplished would lead, unexpectedly, to some of the biggest changes in my life. "I feel dead at the core," I wrote, "and I wonder if I will ever be able to love as I once did. I hope that's just nostalgic bullshit, but that's how it often feels, that I blew my one shot at love. It occurred to me the other night, lying awake in bed, that I may yet experience the greatest love of my life. Strange how imagination occasionally breaks loose and slays doubt with a single blow. Until then, I live with a level of frustration I never thought survivable, wrestling my pillows, waking to nightmares, making love to ghosts."

ABOUT THAT TIME, I drew up a timeline or "life-map" of the past two years. I taped three letter-sized pieces of paper together in landscape format, drew a single line of ink across the horizon about an inch and a half from the top, and began to notate, in chronological order, to the best of my memory, everything I had done and everything significant that had happened since my return from Dallas. I needed to ascertain some pattern or recognizable trajectory to my life. I needed to see the view from thirty-thousand feet, so to speak.

I wound up drawing a second black line lengthwise across the middle of the page, beginning at the halfway point and extending all the way to the end of the timeline, where it tapered out into a series of dashes and ended at the hollow outline of a huge question mark. The upper timeline became, from the point of my MFA applications onward, everything that I had *thought* would happen, including in April, 2011, my possible acceptance into a program, and by August, my move to to another city and matriculation into the graduate school. Instead, what actually happened, as indicated by a big downward arrow aimed at the second time-line, were the events I listed there, making tick marks about an inch apart and labeling the months, then carefully drawing boxes around short phrases like "The Storm" or "Alaska for 3 weeks," and drawing smaller arrows from the corner of the boxes to the point on the timeline where I estimated they had occurred.

By the time it was complete, I was stunned to see just how much had transpired those past two years. I drew a huge X of mul-tiple lines, like the intersecting tracks of a railroad junction, at the point where the crossroads had truly been, the point where my life had painfully divided, as it were, into two possible worlds: one in which I was happily ensconced in a graduate writing program, and another that dead-ended at a mark of the interrogative so large as to pose a question only God could answer.

I still could not imagine where my life was headed. I saw where I had been, though, the trail behind me along a mountain range rambling into the distance. I believed that a sovereign God was capable of using even my sins and painful detours to accom-plish all his purposes for me, but what in the world was I being prepared for? What strange future must await if this were the pre-paratory school for it?

I applied for a job working at a call center downtown and an-other as an inspector for an insurance company, all without suc-cess. Even the Norfolk and Southern Railroad would not give me the chance to work for them all the live-long day. "Roanoke and I have the same relationship as Houdini and his chains," I wrote in my journal. "I have to do something to get out of my parents' house and get on with my life."

An old friend in Arlington, Texas, Jason Myers, (the same friend who'd turned me into the police when I "went nuts," as my pharmacist friend liked to put it) now divorced, offered me a room in his house rent-free while I got back on my feet. It was hard to explain to him that I was actually too broke to even make a cross-country move. I remember reading somewhere about cer-tain saloons in the Wild West, how if you gambled away every-thing, including the clothes off your back, they would issue you a paper suit to wear until your fortunes changed. That's where I found myself, wearing that paper suit.

Cordyceps continued to be a tiny bright spot that winter, selling ninety-five copies its second month. Still, I was under no illusion that my modest sales, however encouraging, were poised to save me financially or catapult me into success. As it turned out, what *Cordyceps* would accomplish was far stranger and better than that.

I BEGAN A NEW journal at the end of February, reluctantly putting pen to paper on the first blank page of a green, leather-bound volume that had been a gift from my ex-girlfriend the previous year. It seemed a thing imbued with bad juju at the time, and I had even tried to return it to the bookstore where I thought she'd bought it, but when they scanned the barcode it didn't show up in their inventory, so there I was, stuck with it.

I took it to the coffee shop and sat down with a cup of Darjeeling on which I calculated I had just spent about 5% of my net worth. I had some royalty money coming to me from *Cordyceps*, but the first check wouldn't arrive for another month. The fifty dollars I had left were from a load of scrap steel I salvaged from around the farm, along with a trash bag full of beer cans I picked up along the roadside in the Jefferson National Forest.

I quickly slid into sarcasm, lampooning the romantic optimism I'd often evinced at the outset of my other journals: "It does merit some introduction, considering how many hours it takes to fill the pages of a journal like this, what travail we are setting upon, what ponderous moments of grim introspection, what inadvertent prophecies and fateful galvanizations, what lugubrious confessions and grandiloquent balderdash we have to look forward to, dear reader!"

I did venture to admit, though, that it had been exciting to meet, for the past two days, my goal of selling ten copies a day (enough royalties to pay my basic monthly expenses), enabling me to "glimpse a reality where I could actually get up in the morning and work single-mindedly on the next novel—without a kind of reckless abandon in ignoring practical concerns..."

A couple weeks later, inspired by rising sales, I began brainstorming a second and third book to turn *Cordyceps* into a trilogy. In March, my sales tripled, and even my father—my father who had warned me all my life that it was all but impossible to make a living as a writer—even he began routinely asking how many books I'd sold on a given day, reading *Cordyceps* for himself sitting on a barstool in the kitchen, using the Kindle app on my mother's laptop, so engrossed he occasionally reached for the computer screen in an effort to turn the page—his first e-book.

By the second week in April, I had written the first sixteen thousand words of the sequel, *Cordyceps Resurgentis.* "It has been a real pleasure getting back into the magic and immersion of writing a novel," I journalled. "Hardly a moment in the day goes by—driving across town, working out at the gym, showering—when I'm not thinking about it, wondering what happens next, imagining various scenarios, talking to myself in the voices of my characters to try out various lines of dialogue. When I'm writing I think in sentences about everything: how I would describe someone I see at the café, the peculiar way someone did something, some quirk of body language. Everything I see or hear has potential for inclusion, or is simply a kind of descriptive practice, strengthening that habit of translating life into words. It's when you overhear a snatch of conversation, and realize you're seeing it as text in your head, even debating where, exactly, you would place the comma to capture the particular nuance—that's when you know you're writing."

The previous month, I calculated, *Cordyceps* had earned the same amount I once made standing behind the front desk of the Baylor Tom Landry Fitness Center for 160 hours. "It has been especially satisfying," I wrote, "on those days when I am selling enough books to focus on writing the sequel and not bother looking for another job. Only another writer would appreciate what a personal victory this is: getting up and brewing your coffee and opening your laptop and paging through a legal pad full of wild notes and arrows, timelines, and doodles from your most outlandish daydreams—and then to think that this is no longer some crazy delusion, no longer just plotting car chases in your pajamas and writing stories in lieu of getting a 'real job.' You're getting paid to do this. You're a professional now. Your crazy daydreams are actually good enough that people all over the world are reading them. Let me tell you, that is a satisfying feeling."

The only drawback to my newfound confidence was that it was based on sales numbers that frequently roller-coastered, tugging my confidence skyward one day and plunging it earthward the next. The future was anything but assured. For all I knew, sales might simply stop, and I had no marketing budget, no publicist, no ad campaign, no book tour to attempt to revive them. My parents' farm was for sale to mitigate the losses they had suffered in the recession, and if necessary the house would be next, possibly ending the living arrangement, which, if I really considered it, was the one thing making my lifestyle possible.

The more frustrated I got, the more I worked on my new novel and the more I hiked. By the end of April, I had completed one hundred pages of *Resurgentis*, and had been hiking Cove Mountain nearly every other day, confessing to my journal that the highest pinnacle at Dragon's Tooth was the only place I could relax.

"It's been a warm spring and I'm already tanned. At night sometimes I look in the mirror at my body, sunburned and lean, a stranger to myself and the few women that have known me, my hair grown long and my beard wild, because the $26.00 haircut and $6.00 for shaving cream is money I don't absolutely have to spend, or because I don't care or because it hardly matters. Late at night, when I'm alone with my ghosts, I consider emailing them or texting them some nostalgic apology, begin to think, perhaps, that the issues that broke us up couldn't possibly be so bad as getting in bed, night after night, alone. But then I realize—or at least decide—that this is a terrible idea that cannot possibly benefit me or them, and that I am only starving for love. I don't know how much longer I can live like this. I don't want to think of life as something to be endured. Maybe I am learning the meaning of perseverance. I am what continues."

MY WRITING LIFE was so cloistered and isolated, I found myself going out into the National Forest that spring to socialize. Hikers of some variety were nearly always present on top of Dragon's Tooth, and it wasn't hard to strike up a conversation, particularly since I knew the area so well, and could helpfully point out the names of nearby mountains when I overheard groups of friends speculating to that end.

Justin Hall and I hiked up to do some Trail Magic that first week of May, carrying a bag of ice and bottles of Gatorade and a plastic cooler on which was written, in black marker, "FOR ANY THRU —The Magician's Nephew (good magic)." We set everything up in the shadow of the vertical stone walls at the summit, standing the bottles of Gatorade in the cooler and pouring the ice over them and waiting to see if any Thrus would come struggling up the back side of the mountain, a brutal and nearly continuous five-mile climb from Pickle Branch, which, you may remember, is where Heath and I camped during the storm.

Justin and I made tea and were talking shop about writing and reading some of our work aloud, as though we were the Cove Mountain chapter of the Inklings, when a red-faced Thru in his fifties came panting along, opened the lid to the cooler, and nearly went into hysterics over the Gatorade. His trail name was Strolling Astronomer, and it turned out he worked at the Chandra X-ray Observatory, or rather he worked at the center in Massachusetts that supports it, since the observatory itself is a satellite orbiting the earth.

We talked for a while about X-rays and gamma rays and black holes and the mind-boggling proportions of the solar system, which is itself only a small borough of the universe. We talked about how, if the sun were the size of a basketball, the earth, proportionately, would be a BB thirty-three feet away.

"Does it make you any more convinced that there is a God," I ventured, "knowing what you know about astronomy?"

"Not really," he said, looking around at the dappled light beneath the trees, while, above us in the branches, songbirds offered up centuries-old songs and the leaves exchanged sunlight for the oxygen we breathed and the sun traveled its course through the cloudless sky, bestowing light and grace and growth on the only planet in the universe where such serendipitous conditions were known to exist.

"I mean, all that time—fourteen billion years—anything could happen in that amount of time," he said.

"That's the interesting thing about time and chance," I rejoined. "If something has, mathematically speaking, zero probability of happening, it doesn't matter how much time you add to the equation. If a coin has nothing on its sides, it doesn't matter how many times you flip it—it will never come up heads or tails."

He thanked me for the Gatorade and continued on his way to Maine. It struck me that humanity's perception of the Divine could be so miserable that fourteen billion years of cold dead space could become a more appealing concept than a God who hung the stars in the sky and called them forth by name.

"I don't know if I would have survived the last two years without the Appalachian Trail," I wrote in my journal that night. "It's hard to think about leaving it again—especially for the soulless materialism of city life, but it seems inevitable that I will have to go away again to find a job."

About that time, the Salmon King called to announce he was moving back to Dallas at the end of August, and suggested we split a two-bedroom apartment and turn the city on its head, while he (ostensibly) would work on a PhD program at the seminary and I would write, "but really," I wrote, "we're both returning from the wilderness to remember what it's like to see good-looking women in public and drink European beers on tap at the Gingerman."

I couldn't think of a good reason not to take him up on it. I'd have some royalty checks rolling in about then, enough to pay my first few months of rent, and it was hard to imagine being depressed while rooming with a guy like Joel, equally likely to be found lying on the couch perfecting the art of throat whistling, making side bets during a poker game to see who would have to go jump in the pool with their clothes on, or proposing spontaneous camping trips, the haste and ill-considered nature of which were only an expected part of the adventure.

"It seems there is no more basic prerogative of a man," I wrote, "than to leave his parents' house and go out into the world to seek his own."

THE GOOD MAGIC OF COVE MOUNTAIN seemed even stronger than usual that spring. I was out doing Trail Magic when I hit it off with an interesting group of friends on the summit. I had been sitting on the uppermost rock, and had called down to a particularly nice-looking girl that, "The view's even better up here." (A line I thought even Joel would be proud of.) I had expected her to politely demur and make some remark such as, Oh, this is quite far enough for me, thank you very much, but instead she actually climbed up the last few feet of the tooth, watching her footing and gripping the rock, and joined me on the summit. She was with a group of five others, who, it turned out, were all believers. We discovered that my graphic designer was a mutual friend, and another of the girls was enrolled in a creative writing program at Baylor University in Waco. I followed them down the mountain like a lost puppy dog, making conversation all the way, and when we got to the parking lot they invited me to join them for dinner at an Indian restaurant in downtown Roanoke. The seven of us gathered around a big table, passing naan bread and asking questions and laughing when the girls said they had speculated among themselves on the way to the restaurant whether or not I was some famous actor, hiding from his fame on the mountain.

I wrote about it in my journal late that night, marveling over how much more extroverted I had become, how the Trail Magic ministry seemed to have reprogrammed my mind. "I used to go hiking only for myself, alone and keeping to myself. Now I go out seeking thru-hikers with confidence and joy—confidence in what I have to give them and joy to meet them, to bless them with cold drinks and fruit and snacks, joy to hear their stories of the trail and life, joy to share God's generosity with them. I have been, in one lifetime—in the space of two years, even—as different as two distinct men climbing that mountain. Perhaps I am finally healed from the woes I brought there two years ago. More than two-hundred hikes later, I feel that I am ready to either move on or stay, that I could finally be content with either. It also helps my overall sense of magnanimity that I sold nineteen books today. This will be the first paycheck I receive in Texas if I decide to go—these are the very sales that might pay my rent at the Marquis on Gaston or buy me a draft beer at the Elbow Room."

Little did I know, the good magic of Cove Mountain was about to change all that.

THIS IS HOW IT happened. I recounted the story in a journal entry titled "Serious Threats to My Hermitage." "I might as well just come out with it. I met an incredible woman. A life-changing woman. Not those girls I mentioned in my last entry—forget them. Those conversations only served to lure me from my self-imposed isolation and awaken my desire to meet a godly woman."

I was at the coffee shop in downtown Salem—not just once, but several times, sitting at my favorite table in the brick doorway, working on *Cordyceps Resurgentis* and perfecting my monastic lifestyle when I noticed a new blonde working behind the counter, tall and lithe, with a way of walking across the café that was nearly the complete undoing of my concentration. Perhaps only by chance—has chance ever really been operative in my life?—by whatever design, I should say, I never had occasion to speak with her, as someone else would wind up taking my order, usually a wise-guy named Ethan who called me "Alaska" and had made a hobby of heckling me at the register. I could tell, though, as I watched her from my table in the back, that she had a great personality, just by the way she laughed when the regulars would chat with her across the counter, something generous about her easy laugh, the way she would throw her head back in hilarity.

But the monastic lifestyle, you see, is one of unwavering devotion. I kept writing.

Maybe a week later, after Ethan had effectively ribbed me about the intensity of my wild hair—"devil horns" he called them—I decided to shave off my beard and cut my hair. (I had told Ethan, with bombastic good humor—and a glance at the blonde filling an airpot nearby—to just wait, as I was going to shock him by shaving my entire head.) I settled, instead, for a shave and a clean-cut fade.

Perhaps a week later, I was clambering over rocks on the summit of Dragon's Tooth—at the spot right before you turn the corner into the gap between the "teeth" and must either begin scaling the rocks or duck beneath a boulder wedged there and climb up through a natural chimney. I was sweating and breathing hard from the climb, feeling a bit naked without my trail beard, when I looked up and saw the rhododendron shaking. From around the corner of the rock—but visually, it seemed, from nowhere at all—stepped a tall blonde wearing a t-shirt and shorts and a small nylon book bag of the kind college students and day hikers often carry. She was long-limbed, her hair almost auburn in that light, and her face when she met my eyes solemn to the near point of fear, her mouth set in a firm line, as one might regard a wild animal not quite known to be safe.

For some reason, the image of her standing on the rock by the rhododendron stamped itself indelibly on my mind—strange because I have seen hundreds, perhaps thousands of day hikers on that mountain that made no such impression. It was a moment. I did not recognize her so far removed from the context of the coffee shop, and it turns out she hardly recognized me in my clean-shaven state. It was the first moment we truly saw each other.

I only nodded curtly and said, "How's it going?" before moving right along on my routine path up to the highest rock. About halfway up, I heard a voice shouting to me, "Hey, don't you come in to the coffee shop?"

It wasn't her. The voice belonged to another barista from the coffee shop that had made tea for me before: a shorter blonde, gregarious and good-natured. We had a brief exchange—me on the summit and they standing in the sandy arena perhaps thirty feet below. Nothing significant. Oh, hey, how's it going? Have you been here before? Yeah, it's great. I come here all the time—that kind of thing. They had another friend with them and the three made their way up the trail single file, talking and laughing as they passed over the hill into the pines out of sight, and I was left to my solitary musings.

Perhaps a week later, I was at the coffee shop and the blonde (the mysterious one from the mountain) was grinding coffee beans at the end of the counter, filling little brown paper bags and folding down the tops with an efficiency that bordered on mechanization. As I was leaving, I made a point of getting up and taking my dishes to the bus pan at the precise moment that she was nearly finished grinding a bag, so that I could casually say something without the din of all that grinding drowning out my low voice. Even monks can be sly.

Nothing much came of it. I introduced myself and apologized for not recognizing her on the mountain. Her name was Allison. My name was Ian. She liked to hike and she and some of her friends were planning to hike the Old Hotel Trail near Buena Vista. All this while she continued to pour coffee beans into the top of the commercial grinder, grinding and slapping the side of the machine to knock the grounds down into the bag, only glancing at me occasionally as we talked, and I supposed that either she was not so much interested in talking to me or that the world would explode if those bags of coffee were not ground immediately.

"I have to tell you," I later wrote in my journal, "it's not so flattering when a girl diverts her attention from you to whack the heel of her hand against the side of a commercial coffee bean grinder. That was our first conversation. Distracted, over the roar of coffee beans being pulverized into tiny, steepable shards. Oh well. I said it was nice meeting her and walked out into the dark and got in my jeep and left."

FIFTEEN MONTHS LATER, we were married. (Turns out I slightly misread that conversation at the coffee grinder.) Of course, it wasn't as easy as that first sentence makes it sound; it was both more difficult and more rewarding than any courtship I might have imagined. But at first it was only fun, as any true comedy should begin.

As Providence would have it, the next time I holed up in the coffee shop to write, a drenching rainstorm pounded the city, sluicing against the skylight above me like a carwash and greatly reducing the typical number of walk-ins. That gave Allison the chance, while sweeping the floors, to work her way closer and closer to my table. I took out my earbuds and struck up a conversation with her (or at least imagined I was the one initiating it) and we continued every time she returned to my table after having to go ring someone up or make a latté.

It quickly became a very intriguing conversation, both because of her subtle cooperation, and because of the peculiar phrases she used, almost as members of some secret underground might drop certain code words to discretely reveal themselves to other devotees, phrases like "if you're where you're supposed to be in life," and who, I wondered, but a Christian would use a phrase like that? Curious, I asked her if she was a believer (not knowing that she had already stalked me on Facebook, ascertained the same about me, and was only trying to lead me to the same realization about her without revealing her source) and she said she was, what turned out to be the first of many surprises, "as though at last God had relented," I wrote in my journal later that summer, "and brought a woman so perfect for me that every one of her attributes was, as it were, a soothing balm for the wounds and disappointments that had come before."

I asked her out for sushi, but she was unable to go because she was working nights, which, at the beginning of a relationship, always puts the guy in the compromised position of seeming over-eager if, for instance, he counters by whipping out a calendar and saying, "What about the night of the 24th? No? How about the 26th? Are you doing anything then?" I decided to play it cool, even though I hated that sense of lost initiative I was all too familiar with from lost games of chess. I had played my gambit. Now I would simply have to wait.

In the meantime, we began a casual correspondence on Facebook, which largely consisted of her peppering me with questions, many of which went unanswered during a busy week when I was remodeling a kitchen about an hour outside of town. She texted me late one night, just as I was getting sleepy, and said, "Just a heads up, I am considering grabbing a beer after work and you'd be welcome to join if you like. I'll need answers to all those questions of mine eventually."

I had spent a long day pounding out ten difficult pages of *Resurgentis,* a particularly violent onslaught of zombies, and from the sound of it, I'd be joining Allison and a handful of her coworkers, I guessed, in a noisy bar where my low voice would barely carry above the general commotion, and I'd probably wind up with someone between us and then I'd have to sit there generating thoughtful questions like an investigative journalist for at least an hour just to be polite. But I couldn't say no.

I got in my jeep and drove across the Colorado Street bridge into Salem feeling depleted and almost entirely devoid of charm and gregariousness. I prayed as I drove, casting myself upon the grace of God. If this turned out to be something like an actual date, and if that date was to be the beginning of a relationship that was his will, then he would just have to empower me to be funny and charming.

The restaurant was on Main Street only a half-block from Roanoke College, a drinking establishment of the kind with old canoes and bicycles hanging from the ceiling and random black and white photos and all manner of quirky estate-sale kitsch screwed to the walls—not a chain restaurant, but the local imitation of one, and its survival in a place like Salem probably owed more to the fidelity of the town than the superiority of its club sandwiches and pretzels dipped in ranch dressing or the handful of domestic brews on tap.

The next surprise was finding Allison waiting in a booth in the back, delightfully and completely alone. She wore a pastel green t-shirt that brought out the brightness of her blue eyes, I couldn't help but notice, as I sat across from her sipping the foam off the top of a draft Fat Tire. What followed was—and I only realized this upon relating it to my mother the next day, hesitating before I said it and speaking the words strangely as though I never thought I would hear such a thing coming from my own mouth—*the most fun I'd ever had on a first date.*

Allison was beautiful and responsive, laughing much—a delightful, unaffected laughter—the resonance of true joy. I had the surreal experience of listening to her share her love for the Lord, and the story of how he had worked in her life to save her from sin and draw her to himself. I cannot describe to you the sensation of that goodness and beauty and truth washing over me after having tolerated so much banality from so many ignorant women. It was like going down to the ocean for the first time and letting a breaker roll over you. Everything I had suffered—and to my own shame, tolerated—in other women had only prepared me to appreciate the marvel before me.

❋ ❋ ❋

IF I WERE GOD—and a great deal of misery and discontent-ment in my life has resulted from exactly that mindset—it would have only made sense to bring along a woman like Allison, then continue to increase sales of my books and prosper me financially so I could see my way forward to provide for her and get married, living happily ever after, and so forth.

As it turns out, God, like his patriarchs of old, sometimes cross-es his hands in blessing us. In retrospect, I can see that he was far more interested in the sort of man I was becoming, in a thing Chris-tians call *sanctification*, rather than merely bringing about the completion of my goals and ensuring serendipitous circumstances along the way, which is essentially what men have always wanted from the gods whenever they devise a religion of their own.

Strangely, things seemed to get harder for me rather than eas-ier, and worse rather than better. After four glorious months, my book sales began to taper off dramatically. The downward trend be-came all too obvious. I watched Allison closely for the first signs that she had begun to regard me as a loser, as had happened upon my ruination in front of girlfriends and fiancés so many times be-fore. But Allison was unshakeable in her faithfulness. At times I felt I was trying to talk her out of falling in love with a writer, someone who had chosen a profession in which the average income, if one is honest and forgets the lottery dream for a moment, is actually only about six thousand dollars a year. I believe I sensed almost uncon-sciously that it would have been easier to fail, to lose her and suffer another heartbreak, than it would be to figure out my own destruc-tive patterns, conquer my darkest fears, and achieve an actual vic-tory in my life.

If it hadn't been for her father's careful attention to our rela-tionship, I would have probably ruined it early on, falling into the same patterns of unsustainable intensity and physical passion that had wrecked my previous romances. Every man is given, by God, the prerogative of being an initiator, but lacking self-control and a greater love for others than himself, he becomes merely a firestarter, and at worst, an arsonist.

My experience on Cove Mountain, and my subsequent submission to God had changed me deeply. I had repented of the most obvious of my sexual sins immediately, but I still saw sanctification as a relative matter of personal reform, rather than the pursuit of the absolute standards of an absolutely holy God.

I was shocked to hear myself agreeing, from the outset of our romance, to save kissing for later—much later, like altar-at-the-front-of-the-church later. It wasn't for lack of desire, I can assure you, but precisely because of that desire, and our past mistakes handling fire, so to speak, that we decided it needed to wait. "Love ceases to be a demon only when he ceases to be a god," Denis de Rougemont wisely said, but if you had told me even a year before that I would happily submit to such restrictions, I would have doubtlessly laughed and probably rolled my eyes and called you a fundamentalist and a Pietist, to boot. By my old way of thinking, I would have told you it was an insult to my manhood to spend so much time with a woman without making love to her, as though I were somehow effete, and of course it is the mark of a merely carnal man to take what he wants and despise anyone that troubles his conscience in the matter.

What I found, oddly enough, was that the way of greatest pleasure lay unexpectedly in obedience and self-denial, a way of living that would have appeared, to my old way of thinking, the worst kind of misery and excoriating discipline, the way a four-year old would regard a plate of steaming vegetables. For the first time in my life, there were no lies to be crafted, no secret sins to be hidden. Four months into our relationship, I could honestly write, "I have never been so satisfied to hold so much passion in reserve." I was learning the qualities, not simply of a lover, but of a spiritual leader. I had always imagined marriage, at its best, to be a garden of delights, but I had never realized it would require the discipline of a farmer to sustain it.

☀ ☀ ☀

I GOT A JOB that fall, not because it was ideal, or even because it would solve many of my financial problems, but because regular employment was a pattern-breaking step in the right direction. The arrangement came with the promise that I would be considered for a management position ($700 per week) once I learned the business, but for now it was only a minimum wage shift at the same coffee shop I had frequented to drink tea and people-watch and write in my journals. Allison no longer worked there, but had started an internship as a nutritional counselor at an assisted living facility. She surprised me by being the first customer I ever served, stopping by on her morning commute when the doors opened at 6:30, insisting that I ring her up for a large coffee, perhaps for the strange ceremony that it was now, our places reversed and the entire coffee shop empty, as though it had existed all along for only we two.

I enjoyed the aromas of steaming black coffee and frothing milk, tea leaves in glass canisters, and breakfast plates under heat lamps at the short order window. It was ridiculously easy, too, compared to the work I had been doing the first month I dated Allison, working in a full-face respirator in the summer heat while obliterating cinderblock walls with a sledge hammer.

I quickly began to appreciate the difference between having work and having a *job*. Employment came with a certain dignity, rising from bed in the dark and putting on the clothes I had washed and hung up to dry the day before, driving across town and parking behind the coffee shop, seeing lights on the church steeples and mist under the streetlights, letting myself in with the key entrusted to me, finding my time card on the door to the manager's office and punching in at the timeclock, a satisfying *chunk* and the stamp in bold ink, one minute before six.

Within a month, it became apparent that I was unlikely to win the favor of the current manager or secure her job when she left to return to college, passing that salaried position like a baton to whomever she pleased. It didn't help matters that I was nearly old enough to be her father. She needled me about the way I swept floors and she criticized the way I washed dishes—too thoroughly, she said—scrubbing each plate instead of simply pushing racks through the sanitizer and restacking them in the kitchen still bearing a film of food residue. Things came to loggerheads one day when I told her I had heard a customer complaining that the cake samples she had set out in little toothpick-impaled cubes tasted stale (almost as though they had been sliced from a cake that had been left in the walk-in freezer since the previous presidential administration) and she had first looked at me with shock, and then replied, as though I were daft, "That's why they're *free*."

She sent me home early many days simply to cut costs, which felt like a punishment when I needed every dollar so badly, and she sent me into the storeroom to scrub sour milk and cigarette butts from the interior of an old chest freezer, and she probably couldn't imagine why I kept showing up for work. Unlike her, I had the advantage of being old enough to have seen Richard Gere doing push ups in the rain in *An Officer and a Gentleman*, while Louis Gossett Jr. shouted in his face, "WHY WON'T YOU JUST QUIT?!"

That is not to suggest I was impervious to discouragement. "At times I have asked God how thoroughly I need to be humbled," I wrote in my journal, "but I have not yet begun to approach the humility of Christ, who humbled himself even to the point of death on a cross."

Working in the service industry was harder than I had imagined. I had always considered it—unfairly—to be the refuge of lazy Millennials who didn't want a real job. But now my feet hurt and my spine radiated heat like a sunburn and my hands were so numb I held Allison's hand one night for quite sometime on a drive across town before I realized she was wearing gloves.

"One of the greatest blessings of this season," I wrote, "has been the confidence I have gained in Allison's love. She really loves me. She loves me even jobless and broke, with less than fifty dollars to my name. She loves me exhausted and dehydrated at the end of a long day. She loves me even though my novel hardly sells a copy every other day and even though many of my clothes have holes in them and my car is continually chirping and vibrating and flashing warning lights, on the verge of some imminent breakdown. She loves me even though these things have inevitably added stress to her life. She loves me even though I am a writer with no time to write, a thirty-three-year-old man working a part-time minimum-wage job and living with his parents. She loves me. It has been proven to me in a way that prosperity could have never demonstrated."

MY COFFEE SHOP GIG dried up that January when, after a month of gradually weaning me from the schedule, one shift fewer each succeeding week, I finally walked through the kitchen to check the bulletin board and found the column below my name completely blank.

February—the month by which Allison and I had originally hoped to be engaged—arrived without any new prospects. I applied for jobs with a fervor to suggest completing applications was the goal in itself. I calculated, at one point, that I had applied for over a hundred jobs since my return from Texas.

I made the most of that newfound abundance of spare time, finishing *Cordyceps Resurgentis* in an intense spate of writing, often sitting at the Starbucks on West Main Street in Salem every day for five and six-hour stretches, getting up only for refills and restroom breaks. My friend Ben Carroll was a manager there and told me the whole staff was intrigued by how long I could sit absolutely still, moving only my fingers.

The day I finished the draft, I bought a four-pack of Guinness and Allison raised a pint with me—a far cry better than my lonely celebration upon finishing the first book. When I was finally done with the editing, my throat sore from reading aloud day after day, and my eye twitching from exhaustion, Allison took me out for a dinner of stuffed ravioli to celebrate getting her boyfriend back.

The low point, as I remember it, came one morning attempting to repair an old tub saw so I could complete a kitchen tile job. I had perhaps two-hundred dollars at the time, another twenty dollars of coins in a jar, and a five-dollar bill I had folded and stashed inside my phone case—my only emergency fund. The problem was with the plastic basin, which was shattered on one corner and would not hold water. I spent an hour wrestling with metal flashing and glue and was beyond ready to give up, but I could not afford to replace the basin or rent another saw. Every dollar counted.

At a certain point of poverty, everything you do begins to seem like a parable. I wondered, bitterly, if that was the place God wanted me to reach, to simply sit down and refuse to go on, refuse to participate in any further acts of pathetic desperation. I wiped the glue from my hands and dialed the customer to explain what was taking so long. I got a pre-recorded message informing me that my cell phone had been disconnected due to an overdue balance of $120, which I had postponed, not knowing where my next paycheck was coming from, or how much I would make on the tile job, which was only paying fifteen dollars an hour.

Bending over that tile saw—sculpting, really, with sheet metal and a length of copper supply line for an armature, I said aloud: "I refuse to accept defeat." I slathered the whole mess with silicone caulk and amazingly it held water all afternoon, even without having properly dried, my efforts to speed along the process with a heat gun only bubbling the silicone into a sticky spittle. The metaphor of the tub saw was an apt one for the state of my finances: patched together and barely holding water.

I worked through the afternoon in a state of frustration, unable to message Allison or take time to sort things out with AT&T, making meticulous cuts on the tile saw with a dull blade and forcing myself to concentrate lest I lose a finger to some careless motion. Later that afternoon, once I had called AT&T from the customer's land line and paid the bill (leaving me with perhaps fifty dollars after my car insurance auto-draft went through) I got my phone working and saw that Allison had messaged me something about a promising job lead. But there had been so many of those. I penciled the number down on the ripped-off corner of a cardboard box and dialed it, leaving a voicemail for the manager of a local bottled water company that might be hiring a delivery driver. I heard nothing back for the rest of the evening, working on the tile job until seven o' clock that night. It was only another long shot, and there had been so many longshots and misses before.

A cold rain was falling the next morning when I went to finish the tile job, and I sat in my jeep with my head against the steering wheel for a while before I went in. February has always been a hard month for me, to the point that I have, at times, had to fight an almost superstitious fear of it coming around again on the calendar. February was the month of my commitment in Fort Worth, the worst month of my graduate school rejections, and even without those painful anniversaries it was always the point in winter when my nerve damage hurt the most and it seemed that spring would never come.

The final indignity that morning was getting a fragment of rubber glove stuck in my zipper, so irrevocably that I resorted to holding my fly shut with long, horizontal strips of painter's tape. Such was my condition when I dialed the bottled water company again, this time getting the Roanoke manager on the phone in person, and shocked to hear him say he wanted me to come in the next morning at nine a.m. for an interview. I hastily wrote down the directions to the warehouse on another piece of cardboard box, thanked him, and hung up. I knelt there on the kitchen floor beside a gooey bucket of mortar, tears in my eyes. It had been four months since my last interview.

＊ ＊ ＊

THE INTERVIEW WAS IN the warehouse district in southeast Roanoke, only blocks from the place, now a ruin, where my great grandfather had once operated a coal shovel for the railroad. I wore a button-up shirt and a nice pair of slacks—nothing *too* nice, no tie, trying not to look too corporate, as though I couldn't throw a fifty-pound bottle of water over my shoulder, or as though I might consider myself above manual labor. I went in with my sleeves rolled up.

I was directed into a cluttered fishbowl office behind towering pallets of water bottles. File boxes and defunct office equipment crowded the room. Yellow sticky notes and papers written in product code were pasted and taped to nearly every surface.

I liked my interviewer at once: a muscular, red-bearded man with honest, clear eyes, and a demeanor about the office of a man who had only reluctantly entered management, who would have preferred the simplicity of physical labor to inventory and personnel management and telephone calls. He read me a list of benefits and what he called "expectations" from a sheet of hand-written notes. The job would pay thirty-five to forty-five thousand a year, which I accepted with a stoic nod that did not begin to admit the dreamlike quality of it after so many years scraping by. He assured me the work was hard, but he looked me over and said I seemed to be in good condition. I told him I liked to split firewood for fun.

The regional manager happened to be there as well, an older man in his late fifties, bald and thick-necked, with the same chest and shoulders everyone at the warehouse seemed to have. He sat down and regarded me with eyes that were hard, but keen and discerning. He asked me to tell him a little bit about my background, and I talked about growing up in construction and being very familiar with hard work and driving various trucks, delivering packages for FedEx (which really seemed to excite them, and only now, in retrospect, can I see how even those few months that seemed so wasted were the Lord's perfect providence in preparing me for the future), my office work, which had confirmed my desire for a more active job, and my experience in a coffee shop, which was good preparation for selling the coffee-related products that they also distributed.

As it turned out, the regional manager had once worked construction himself, and the Roanoke manager had previously worked for his own father, so these two men seemed perfectly prepared to understand my unique background. The regional manager asked what motivated me. I told him I wanted to get married, settle down, and have a normal life. He left the office and returned with a blue polo shirt bearing the Shenandoah Water logo. I was to return in two days for a ride-along with the Roanoke manager so they could see how I worked, and I could learn what the job entailed.

That Friday, I arrived at the warehouse in the dark of the early morning, the big International D-bay truck already rumbling at an idle, warming up, already stocked with more than two hundred five-gallon water bottles. Wes Young, the Roanoke Manager, drove us down 220 south to Martinsville, making conversation as we went. (It started out with small talk, how old are your kids and so on, but by the end of the day we would be ranting about politics, talking guns, and swapping horror stories from various jobs we'd had.)

Our first delivery was to a grocery store. I felt immediate satisfaction, stepping down from the truck wearing the company hat, pulling out the bright blue bottles of clear water and loading them onto the flatbed dolly, wheeling them inside, the cold morning air burning in my nostrils and a pleasant surge of blood in my chest and arms from the work.

We spent the morning making deliveries, offloading nearly half the truck at big box stores before running stops at small businesses and factories, doctor's offices and homes, sometimes using the hand truck to carry five bottles at once, but often just throwing one bottle up on our shoulders and carrying another by the handle like a suitcase. We stopped at a gas station, and while we were waiting for the huge diesel tank to fill, I texted Allison a picture of my hand, filthy from work. A good thing.

Wes had me drive for a while, and I played it cool, bouncing in the air ride seat and slapping the air brake release like a pro, never quite letting on how little experience I had with trucks that size (almost none). I knew it would be stressful and tiring, unloading all that water by myself and having to learn twenty different routes, each with thirty or more stops, but I also knew that nothing could be as stressful as another three years without a steady paycheck.

That afternoon, on our way back to Roanoke, on an otherwise unremarkable stretch of road through Garden City, we had our "little talk" as Wes called it, asking me if I still wanted the job, then telling me I had it and shaking hands with me over the console while he drove, disbelief and elation and relief washing over me, doing my best not to tear up in front of the man. And to think it had all come about because a friend of mine from church, Jeremie Shelor, had parked his Interstate Batteries delivery truck alongside a Shenandoah Water delivery truck, both of them just happening to run the same stop, and striking up a conversation, whereupon my predecessor had told Jeremie he was quitting and going into the catering business. Jeremie urged me to send in my resume, where, I later learned, it had sat unopened in Wes's inbox.

Then Allison remembered someone she used to go to church with, who now worked at a Shenandoah Water facility in northern Virginia. This particular friend just happened to be attending a company-wide meeting when Allison texted him, sitting next to the Roanoke manager himself, to whom he turned and put in a good word for me, and who then told him to tell Allison to have me call him. Got all that?

I picked up my jeep from the warehouse parking lot, stopping only to put twenty dollars of gas in my tank. That morning I had driven to the warehouse on fumes, praying for mercy and hoping it would be an epic finish to my poverty. I drove straight to Allison's parents' house and walked in with the company ball cap hidden in my back waistband. I found Allison in the kitchen baking cookies for that night's bible study. I hugged her and when she asked how it went I pulled out the hat and put it on and said, "I hope you have enough money in your bank account for a good bottle of champagne."

Allison gave a little shriek, fell against me, and cried.

I HIKED COVE MOUNTAIN that weekend, several times having the sensation I had forgotten something, my pack felt so light. But it was only the heavy heart I had carried up that hill so many times. Ten weeks later, Allison agreed to marry me on that very mountain. I took her up to Dragon's Tooth and had her stand on the rock where I had first seen her a year before, and I stood on the same rock I had leapt onto at that very moment when the rhododendron began to shake, and I would have many years and many more hikes to awfully consider that the mind of God had touched upon those very stones; that he had really been *present* there on that mountain for my sake, there to reveal the gift I had sought in vain, with the perfect timing of one fleeting moment: neither an instant too soon or too late for all the circumambulations Allison and I had taken to arrive there. Can you believe, after everything you have read of my life, that it was only coincidence? I cannot.

"I had just stepped up on this rock," I said, directing our little reenactment. "I saw those rhododendron shaking and you stepped out—no, go a little further—you were all the way around the corner."

This time, when Allison brushed past the screen of rhododendron, she saw I had taken a knee on the boulder where I had been standing a moment before, and in my hand was an open velvet box, and inside the box was her grandmother's heirloom sapphire and diamond ring in a new setting. I asked her a question, with tears, and she answered through tears, covering her mouth with both hands as I stepped down from the rock and went to her in two quick strides and took her in my arms. A light rain fell, of which neither of us took any note.

WE WERE MARRIED IN the church on August 31, 2013, a day I can only describe as a magical blur punctuated by moments so intense and beautiful that they seared themselves upon my memory. I wrote in my journal that seeing Allison for the first time in her wedding dress was "perhaps the only thing in my life that has truly stunned me visually: brilliant white in that morning light outside the church, disbelief for a moment that this otherworldly creature regarding me with her head bent curiously and fiery blue eyes could be my Allison and not some being stepped from a glorious dimension.

"In that instant I had many thoughts. I understand now, what the apostles meant when they wrote of angels that their 'appearance was like lightning,' a sight so powerful and bright that it strikes you, and so forcefully that an audible noise seems to accompany it."

That night I told Allison that the vision of her had given me the sensation of what it might be like someday, to find her in heaven, to see her glorified—a glimpse of my wife made holy and pure, her sanctification complete, and that glimpse seemed to serve as a charge to me as a husband, to lead and love her in such a way through this life that I may present her, at last, so adorned as I found her.

Only our closest friends understood what our pastor, Nick Shaffer, meant when, after giving me permission to kiss my bride, he said, "The first kiss is the sweetest." No one they explained it to could believe that we had actually waited. But we had, and so much of the magic of that day was the meaning Allison and I had painfully invested in it all those long months, all those nights saying good-bye and holding her in my arms and finally having to step apart with nothing more than a parting glance; and the satisfaction we had on our wedding day because of that restraint was so intense I later wrote in my journal "that I would have waited another fifteen months for it if I had to."

One of the funniest things happened after we walked the aisle together as man and wife, shaking hands with as many people, it seemed, as the President leaving a State of the Union speech, and were whisked into a little side room by ourselves while everyone cleared out of the sanctuary so the photographer could set up for the family photos to follow, and it was then that our friend Ben Carroll, the barista from the Starbucks where I had written much of *Resurgentis*, went looking for his misplaced wallet and keys and stumbled into that same room where Allison and I were quickly losing count of our second, third, fourth, and fifth kisses, hardly even distracted by Ben's entrance, or the traumatized instant it took him to stammer an apology and flee for his life, horrified and later relating, with full drama, how he had "busted in on Ian and Allison full-on making out."

The reception was held in an open shelter at Camp Alta Mons, the sweat under my starched collar giving it the feel of an old-time summer revival. Allison and I circulated among tables full of friends eager to congratulate us. Even my old friends from seminary had come: Heath Coles as one of my groomsmen, Joel "The Salmon King" Reemtsma as my best man, and Ryan Smith and Scott Grace, who had worked with me at my office job in Texas, and Garrett Mathis, a favorite critic and beta reader, who warned me now, with a solemn wink, not to let all this happiness go to my head, lest it ruin my writing.

We danced in the late summer heat, a live band playing, and in that blur of faces and twinkling white lights it seemed we had called together some vision of the afterlife, of the saints gathered around us, the only requirement for their admission full joy in this union, at last, of bride and groom.

We dashed down a gauntlet of friends who pelted us with diced rosemary and lavender; I remember pulling Allison by the hand, the bustle of her dress lifted in her other hand, taking a full blast right in the mouth as I was yelling something—one surreal and fleeting moment of wild joy. We dove into a Toyota Avalon bedecked with balloons and shoe polished messages streaked across the windows, and we drove home in a late afternoon downpour, cars that passed us tossing whole buckets of water onto the windshield, and only the concentration necessary to not run off the road and kill us could keep me from staring at Allison, so radiant in that dress. We stole kisses at traffic lights with the cascading rain for a veil, and we stole kisses when she leaned close to me while I was driving, as long as I could see the road, and our excitement mounted with each turn that brought us closer to home: Scruggs Road and then Lakewood Forest Road and then turning into the gravel driveway and making a mad dash for the old chain link gate, propping open one side with a stick and the other with a rock, my dress shirt plastered to my skin by the time I got back to the car, breathless, driving the gravel ruts of the farm road, down past the tobacco barns to the cabin, and then another dash through standing water to open her door, then both of us streaking for the porch, splashing through puddles, the rain washing bits of rosemary and lavender down from our hair, little pieces of herbs that we were still finding months later in the couch and for a while in the sheets of the bed—though how they got there must remain for you, dear reader, a mystery dark and sweet as that first kiss itself.

III.

I RARELY MADE IT up to Dragon's Tooth those first years after we were married. I worked as a route driver for seventeen months, daily lifting an average of 30,000 pounds of bottled water, often exhausted and sometimes even falling asleep upright at the dinner table. Down in Bassett, at one of my industrial stops, there was a factory worker that called me his "MMA fighter in training," my effort to unload ninety bottles of water onto a loading dock and then load them again onto hand trucks, twenty-three bottles at a time, pushing a thousand pounds of water across the factory floor—all of it apparently reminding him of a montage from a Rocky movie, Stallone pounding sides of beef or lifting logs in preparation for a big fight. What I might be in training for, though, I could not have begun to imagine.

On the weekends, I sometimes had moments of introspection to wonder if I was still a writer, if that would ever be true again now that I barely had time to read, yet alone write my own books. "What was I supposed to do?" I wondered in my journal, "Never pay my bills, go bankrupt, give up on lasting relationships, all the while demanding that my books sell more copies and gain more recognition? Writing is a miserable obsession. And yet how I long for it. How I long to read and read and fill my mind with sentences, to hear the given line and seize it, to sit before the blank page and feel creativity coiled and live in my mind like a ball of electricity, unspooling and unspooling, word after word, sentence after sentence, page after page, to bring about other worlds, to sense all the passion and mystery of creation."

In retrospect, my attempt to make a living as a novelist seemed like a failed experiment. Now, every time I delivered a case of Folgers Regular I made as much or more than my books did on any given day. Every two months, my sales commission amounted to as much as I had ever made writing. Even my journals lay neglected, sometimes for entire months. All that pensive reflection, all those lonely hours sitting in coffee shops, all that feverish effort to finish manuscripts, all the painstaking editing and polishing and formatting in the hope that the finished product would miraculously change my life—all that seemed nothing more now than a part of my desolate past.

"It didn't work," I insisted. "It's a frustrating and impossible career. On to real life." And then, unexpectedly, one of the most qualified literary critics I knew messaged me saying she had just read *Cordyceps Resurgentis* in three sittings, that it was even better than the first book in her opinion, that she was genuinely shocked and that I was a brilliant writer. Hope crept back in; the dream would not die. It would lie underground, I realized, waiting like a seed, dormant for ten years or a thousand.

ALLISON AND I LIVED in a series of tiny houses: the cabin by the lake, a hundred-year-old second-story apartment, and an attic over a garage, converted into a one-bedroom apartment. Each of those places became home when Allison decorated them, placing a bale of straw and colorful gourds by the door, lighting candles and creating thoughtful arrangements of burlap and pine cones, framing pictures and pages of favorite hymns to hang on the walls, and always, when I came home, filling the house with the aroma of the dinners she prepared.

I remember the first day back from the honeymoon, still disoriented to my new life, sitting at the table in my work uniform shortly after five o' clock in the morning, watching Allison move about the kitchen barefoot in a silk chemise, making coffee, scrambling eggs, stretching on her tip-toes to reach something on the top shelf—the utter marvel of this beautiful woman making my breakfast, as though all the struggle to get to that point could simply be forgotten, that I could wake up one morning and find myself living an entirely different life, married after all those years of going to other friend's weddings, *my own wife* after all those frustrating episodes with girlfriends, all the presumption of women not truly my own; but now I had this woman, completely and rightfully mine, to gaze upon and enjoy for the wonder that she was, not simply a flower, as my favorite college professor, Walter Schultz, once spoke of his own wife, but a bouquet of flowers.

We held to that routine as long as we could, until my back gave out after a particularly difficult week in which I had attempted to run six routes in four days. A series of X-rays revealed my spine and neck were significantly arthritic, and inflamed enough that my doctor placed me under temporary restrictions to lift no more than ten pounds. I asked to be transitioned into a sales job, but the position did not exist and no one seemed able or willing to create it. I had little choice but to serve my notice, my managers providing a temp to ride with me those last two weeks, ostensibly to do my heavy lifting, but actually serving more as welcome source of entertainment: an Alderol-deprived twenty-something, father to "five or six" kids, he told me, pumping both knees in the passenger seat, an aluminum pint of Rip It Fuel in one hand and a burning Pall Mall in the other, occasionally interjecting—in his own stream-of-consciousness dialogue—the particular song playing at that moment in the one white earbud planted on the side of his head, singing lyrics from a wide range of songs that corresponded to nearly anything I said, and very often transforming, in a sort of tortured falsetto, the last line of some chorus into the

Screamo style, at which he was particularly adept, and making a somewhat interesting decision, our last day together, to drop a Vicodin, which had the effect, at least once, of giving him temporary amnesia on our way out of a building, and led to the confession, as he trailed along behind me, "I'm really buzzing right now. I have no memory of this elevator."

Allison and I celebrated our first anniversary in the middle of those two weeks with an epic twenty-mile hike from Troutdale to 311 in Catawba, hiking through rainstorms and the rainbows that appeared afterwards, making tea on the summit of McAfee's Knob, looking back in awe of the long ranges we had traversed together, hiking down the fire road in the dark, holding hands, toads hopping away from us at the approach of my headlamp beam, and star-gazing in the parking lot while we waited for Allison's parents to come pick us up, because we had talked ourselves into going home and making a steak dinner instead of camping out that night.

My first week unemployed we had what you could only call a second honeymoon, Allison saying it felt like she had her husband back, and it was only after I was finally rested that I realized I had quite forgotten what it felt like to not live in a state of constant exhaustion and pain.

"Life is delicious again," I wrote, "like a meal savored rather than eaten in a hurry, sandwich quarters stuffed into your mouth at stoplights, nearly inhaled, still chewing as you carry ninety pounds of water across some customer's lawn to their front door."

ALL THAT REST CAME with a price, though, namely the rapidly diminishing balance in our checking account, what had only been a fear at first but soon became a very concrete and quantifiable countdown to zero. The fact that I had long known my job was physically unsustainable did little to lessen the shock. This was, after all, the job that had been such a personal victory, the job that had enabled me to finally get married and provide for my fledgling new family.

I fought against despairing thoughts that threatened to creep into my mind. I knew all the right things to write in my journal: "I must have faith, stalwart faith, that our God will provide abundantly beyond all that we ask or think." But I couldn't help but feel as though one of the ugly failures of my old life had reached into my newfound happiness and laid hold of me once more.

But I was not the same man I once was. I was learning how to fight, learning that the faithfulness of my thoughts played a big role in defending myself from depression. I was bolstered by the following excerpt from Spurgeon:

"Christian, you ought not to dread the arrival of evil tidings; because, if you are distressed by them, what do you more than other men? Other men have not your God to fly to; they have never proved his faithfulness as you have done, and it is no wonder if they are bowed down with alarm and cowed with fear: but you profess to be of another spirit; you have been begotten again unto a lively hope, and your heart lives in heaven and not on earthly things; now, if you are seen to be distracted as other men, what is the value of that grace which you profess to have received? Where is the dignity of that new nature which you claim to possess?"

I took the canoe Allison had given me for Christmas and paddled against the wind all the way across Carvin's Cove Reservoir and beached it and sat on a shingle of loose shale by a persimmon tree that grew there, heavy-laden with fruit, feeling as though I had ventured to the far end of the world and found the tree of life on that windswept bank. I sat on the shore and found several ripe persimmons, sucking the pumpkin-orange flesh from the skins and spitting out the seeds, staring out over the olive green water and filling several pages in the journal I laid across my knee.

"Whatever reset button there is in a man's mind when he comes to the end of himself, when he is finally not afraid of the adventure that will change his life, I have hit it."

My father graciously lent me the equipment we had once used in our construction business: a diesel truck and trailers, a Bobcat skid steer and an assortment of chainsaws I put to use immediately, learning much about the art of the takedown from my friend Jesse Dunker, who had been climbing trees and running his own landscaping business for nearly fifteen years. One of the first jobs we worked together, I was standing on a customer's roof watching Jesse shimmy along a branch ten feet above me, using a pruning saw to cut off limbs, which I then attempted to catch with a garden rake held over my head.

"I could go get my pole saw," I offered.

"You have a *pole saw*?" Jesse said.

Later that day I noticed that Jesse's trailer was already mounded high with cut branches. "I could go get my dump trailer," I offered.

"You have a *dump trailer*?" Jesse said.

That was how it went in the beginning, how we first realized we might have the makings of a useful partnership. Lumberjacking was hard work, but intermittent enough that I was able to recover somewhat between gigs, and I managed to piece together odd jobs for a year and a half, but I still wasn't making enough to pay our bills, and I continued to cast around for other money-making ideas, including creating print editions of my books and building wine racks from reclaimed lumber, while Allison supplemented our income by working at the compounding pharmacy owned by my chess mentor. We were enjoying our life together, but our relationship was the only aspect of it that bore any sense of permanence; all our efforts to make a living seemed nothing more than a stop-gap measure. The title of one of my journal entries about that time sums up my felt identity: "Rent Hero," someone who manages, somehow, to get another skid steer job off Craigslist or a tree to cut down, or a trench to dig just in time to pay the rent. I felt that I was playing a game of brinkmanship in life, both financially and physically. We couldn't go on indefinitely like this.

Late that February, I was standing at the sink washing dishes while, Ginger, the six-year-old greyhound we had adopted, waited impatiently for me to take her out. Only a few more dishes I couldn't bear to leave for later, but the drying rack was full, a mounded sculpture of downturned dishes. Ginger was growing impatient, practically crossing her legs.

Allison came around the corner into the kitchen and I started to say, "Can you dry these?" but then I looked at her again. She was holding something in her hand, something small and white. Then I noticed the expression on her face: her eyes too wide, and a smile she seemed hesitant to allow to begin. The object she held was slender and oblong with a tiny window in the plastic, a window showing two very tiny pink lines.

"Are you serious?" I remember saying, before I took her in my arms and she folded into me in a way that would seem clichéd, something from a cheesy romance novel, if I even attempted to describe it.

A single moment, and our lives were changed. Some weeks before, unaccounted for by all but God himself, another life had begun in the dark while we slept, while the Maker recalled his stars from the blue twilight outside our windows and the sun rose over a world to which we ourselves were still children.

I WRACKED MY BRAIN that winter for a way to solve what felt like the Rubik's Cube puzzle of my career and financial problems. I was confident that I had been faithful to work the job the Lord had provided, up to the point of serious injury, but why was it that my nascent careers always encountered some insurmountable roadblock? In my life before Christ, it had been plain enough that this was the disciplining hand of God, thwarting me—what seemed like cruelty to my rebellious mind but was actually the kindness of God leading me to repentance—but now I wondered what to make of it. Never had I felt so adrift, so lost.

While Allison was at work, I scoured the internet fruitlessly for a job that might be both physically and financially sustainable.

A countdown had begun on Allison's career; she had already cut back from four days per week at the pharmacy to three, and in another month our rental contract would expire, leaving us with a difficult decision. The thing about having a resume full of jobs I didn't want to repeat was that this was the exact opposite assumption of every career-hunting website and temp agency: key words analyzed and job matches found by helpful but stupid algorithms which could not and would not understand my conundrum.

I was working with Jesse one day, sitting on the roof of a customer's house watching him climb the papery bark of a River Birch, at least thirty feet in the air swaying on limbs no more than a couple inches in diameter—and that was hardly the craziest thing I had seen him do—thinking how insane he was for doing this kind of work for the past fifteen years and how I wouldn't do it for all the money in the world, when he said to me, seemingly from a heart overflowing with pure joy, "I love doing this. I absolutely love it. This is what I was born to do."

I thought to ask him if he had climbed trees as a child, and sure enough, he related stories of free-climbing sixty-foot pines as a teenager, swaying back and forth in storms.

"I was a little bit nuts," he admitted.

I had to admire a man that was making a living doing the thing he loved, smiling about it and reveling in a beautiful day for his work. And of course it made me think, sitting there on that roof, what it might be that *I* was born to do.

Writing, of course. And if that forty-year-old tree climber was crazy enough to keep doing the thing he loved, what excuse did I have for not writing? For not managing my time and resources in such a way that I would be willing even to accept humble circumstances in order to continue doing the thing I loved? The thing that gave me that duck-in-water feeling, as my mom used to say. There had to be a way.

Several times in our married life, Allison and I had discussed the possibility of submitting another round of grad school applications for a program in creative writing. At every crossroads, predictably, maddeningly, and helplessly, this was the realization

I came to, but perhaps it was the very reason why no other career would work. Every time we broached the subject, though, the thought of finding both the time and money for it seemed less feasible than ever.

I hatched a crazy plan and ruminated on it for a month before I had the courage to mention it to Allison. It was an idea we had touched on before, but only in terms of a worst-case scenario, as in, if everything goes to pot and there's a nuclear war, we could always move in with one of our parents. Had it really come to that? To even consider such a thing felt like I was backsliding into childhood, boomeranging once again, only now with a wife in tow, and apparently nothing at all left of my pride in being an independent adult.

Several hundred feet from my parents' house was a detached six-car garage with a staircase leading up to perhaps four hundred square feet of living space built into the attic between the sloping roof rafters—a true garret—currently unfinished with nothing but plywood on the floors and drywall yellowing in the slow passage of sunlight over those walls, dawn to dark, for a decade. I began praying that the Lord would prepare Allison's heart to hear what I had to say and receive it well. Until then, I had never imagined that it would be possible to serve as the spiritual leader of my home without a more certain vision of our future. What I learned was that leading didn't necessarily imply I had life by the horns; but it did require, at least, that I acknowledge my responsibility for the fact that life does, indeed, have some very intimidating horns and that I was the one that needed to figure out how we might lay hold of them.

Allison shocked me one night by bringing up the subject herself, after reading the blog post of a woman whose family had lived with her parents for a while during hard times. I finally told her that I had thought of a way we might reduce our living expenses, perhaps giving my contracting business time to gain traction and possibly even putting us in a position where grad school would be feasible. All it involved was moving into an unfinished living space the size of an RV with no indoor plumbing, bathroom, or kitchen, and which happened to be infested, at present, with a well-established population of mice. While pregnant.

Surprisingly, she did not divorce me. This was, of course, the same woman who had refused to give up on a broke-back fiction writer, who had adapted to a cabin in the woods with a dishwasher that did not work and whose iron-laden well water turned her hair orange, the same woman who had cheerfully accepted the confines of the makeshift kitchen in our second apartment, preparing gourmet meals on perhaps three feet of countertop, making do with drawers that stuck, which she learned to close with a well-swung hip, and never complaining about having a single lower cabinet, but instead inventing ways of nesting our pots and pans like Russian dolls. This, too, she would take in stride.

We sat down with my parents to explain our predicament, and they generously offered to provide the materials necessary to finish the living space over the garage, even buying us sharp-looking stainless steel appliances for the kitchen. I brought all my old construction skills out of retirement and managed to finish the bedroom before we moved in, and I still marvel over my wife's resilience to the primitive conditions we lived in those first months, stuffing a bath towel under the bedroom door at night to keep the mice out, and squatting over a little pump-action camp toilet in the hallway until I could build a bathroom and dig trenches for the sewer connection outside.

"I know that I could make my home anywhere that I took her," I wrote, "that any room she graces with her touch will glow with the warmth of a home, and that the one and only irreducible necessity of our home, no matter where we might make it, no matter where the future finds us, is that we are together. A good marriage is its own shelter from the world. It requires no more; it admits to no less. It is enough."

✳ ✳ ✳

MY FIRST SON, Phinehas Cove Duncan, (named after the mountain, of course) was born that fall, and I began to imagine a cozy, domestic life, a cottage industry I described in my journal as a "beautiful, hazy dream" wherein I would work in the garage below the house making things with my hands, wine racks and furniture from reclaimed lumber, and we would sell them at the local farmer's market on Saturday mornings along with the soaps and candles and granola that Allison made.

But it was a dream I was unable to bring to fruition, no matter how hard I labored over my projects. We sold a few pieces here and there, but nothing that began to pay anything like wages for the time I had invested. I set up my wares at a wine festival that fall, watching, from beneath my plastic-wrapped booth, a record-breaking eight inches of rain turn the concourses into goo while drunken festival-goers mud-wrestled and bought no wine racks whatsoever.

All of my recent contracting bids had not panned out. None of the furniture I'd driven to Richmond and displayed in a shop in Cary Town had sold. We were starting to receive cut-off notices for our electricity and cell phones, and I had already failed to renew my general liability insurance. Besides all that, tendonitis in my right arm had rendered it almost useless. A sober assessment of my profits and losses led to the conclusion that I sucked at running my own business. Once again, I needed a job.

I was helping my tree climbing friend with a tile job at his house when I decided to drop my resume off at a big gun store that was hiring. I put it off the first day and almost blew it off the second, once I got to thinking, since it was only a part time sales position, after all, and unlikely to pay much, and forty-five minutes from my house to boot. For some reason that day, I just gave up overthinking everything and stopped in. I submitted my resume, filled out a paper application, and made small talk with one of the sales staff. I went home. Probably nothing would come of it.

A week later, they called me for an interview, and two weeks after that, after I had quite given up on it, they called to tell me I had the job. I sailed through all the background checks and got my sales numbers from the Virginia State Police. It was only part-time for the first two months, but the owners seemed to like me and soon promoted me to full-time hours and gave me a key to the building. Even full-time hours didn't amount to a lot of take-home pay in the retail industry, but Allison continued to clean houses and I took the occasional side job on Saturdays, and somehow we made it work. We believed in the company and trusted that I would be promoted eventually, and that it would be worth the wait. And, for the first time in our married life, it felt as though we had a sustainable lifestyle. Allison would sometimes surprise me in the afternoons, bringing me a cup of coffee, carrying my son onto the sales floor in his car seat so I could make googly faces at him and earn one of his big grins, and even though gradu-ate school was still a distant dream, at least now I wasn't destroy-ing my body.

We still struggled to survive on my paychecks, even after I was promoted to assistant manager. "It is painful to watch Allison," I wrote, "already exhausted from taking care of Phin and maintain-ing our household and cooking every meal, casting about for ideas to make additional income, when really there is no additional time or energy with which to make it."

I kept Phin on my days off while Allison cleaned houses, com-ing to cherish that time to revel in my son, then seven months old. "I could stare at him in wonder all day," I wrote, "for all that he is, and all that he represents." And on another day: "I have not recently laughed so much as I have today, trying to change his di-aper and put fresh clothes on him, which is like trying to change the outfit of a miniature person intent on pantomiming the Amer-ican Crawl."

That April, Allison and I hiked up to Dragon's Tooth for the first time with Phin, riding in the baby carrier, he and I wearing matching blue bandanas, Rambo-wrap style, drawing grins and compliments from other hikers on the trail.

It had been five years since Heath and I had come down from that mountain. "My life since then has been wonderful and often miraculous," I wrote. "I have a beautiful wife and son and a peaceful home. I have been granted, without riches, the very things wealthy men often wish they could trade their riches for."

✳ ✳ ✳

TOWARD THE END OF MAY, I decided I could afford to make use of my employee discount and buy a little Glock nine-millimeter for Allison. I had recently won a sales competition and as my prize, the owner was pitching in an additional one hundred and fifty dollars toward the cost. Eight years had passed since I had purchased a new firearm. You might imagine my surprise then, when one of my coworkers submitted the background check online, (naturally you're not allowed to process your own paperwork) only to have the Virginia State Police call to ask if this Ian Duncan character might still be loitering in the showroom. One of my coworkers came to tell me, her face frozen into a solemn mask.

I had often worked with the police to distract and detain legally disqualified gun purchasers (without realizing they were being detained) until an officer could get to the store to give them a stern talking to, and sometimes (while we pretended not to watch) take them into custody. All of us there at the store helped the police hold the line against illegal gun purchasers. FBI agents, Roanoke City Police, Virginia State Police: all of them treated us like friends and allies.

"You're Ian Duncan?" the officer asked over the phone, sounding nearly as confused as I was.

"I'm the assistant manager here," I said.

"Wait, you *work* there?"

And so on. He was sending someone to talk to me, he said. I hung up the receiver. My coworker wanted to know what in the world was happening. I offered a strained smile. "Some of my past sins have caught up with me," I said.

I shook hands with the gray uniformed officer of the Virginia State Police, who definitely glanced apprehensively at the holstered Glock on my hip, while the owner of the company ushered us out of sight to a private conference room. We settled in, and a lot of head-scratching ensued.

"Have you ever been committed to a mental institution?" the officer finally thought to ask.

Well, as a matter of fact, I had, I admitted, but that was ancient history—sixteen years ago. Wasn't there a legal sunset on the firearms disabilities created by involuntary commitments? I'd always been told it was seven years.

More head scratching. Bear in mind that I was often the only manager present at a Class III NFA firearms dealer, personally responsible for an entire showroom stocked with guns and ammunition, including a safe full of silencers and a number of fully automatic machine guns. I had passed the most extensive background checks the State of Virginia could muster. They even had my fingerprints on file.

I quickly got the impression, from the look on the officer's face, that he fully anticipated that somewhere along the chain of command, one of his superior's heads might explode over this. He would have been within the law to arrest me immediately. Instead, he took up the mystery eagerly, pulling out his personal cell phone and making a number of calls, reaching out to a contact he had at the probate court in Tarrant County, Texas, to attempt to ascertain how it had all happened and what it now meant for me legally. Plenty of his questions I didn't even know how to answer about my commitment; after all, I'd been essentially nuts when they hospitalized me, and drugged out of my mind when they let me go. I was understandably fuzzy on the details.

We finally spoke to an attorney that specialized in firearms law, who informed us, over speakerphone, that however I might have slipped through the cracks of the system, I was to be considered, for all practical purposes, the same as a felon, and could not legally possess or even handle firearms, let alone continue to sell them. It would probably be best if I left the building immediately.

The owner assured me we would get to the bottom of it, that we would get it resolved quickly, but I knew better than he, with an old dread long suppressed, that if it were possible at all it would be a long and difficult process.

I WALKED OUT OF the gun store showroom that afternoon, not knowing how long it would be, if ever, before I was able to return. I had worked hard and earned the trust of the owners, and more importantly to me, I actually liked them. It wasn't just a gun store; a multi-million-dollar indoor firing range was under construction which I had helped, in part, to build; a second location was being proposed in another city, and the company was quickly becoming a hub for training and education. I had invested six months in my advancement from a part-time sales position to full-time management. I had found a home in a rapidly-growing company, with many more opportunities for advancement forthcoming. Just that morning, I could say I had a good job that I enjoyed; a few hours later I did not. A few hours earlier, I had supervised an entire showroom full of weapons and ammunition; now, if I was discovered with so much as a single round of .22 rimfire rattling in my pocket among my loose change, I could go to jail.

Anything could have happened those first two weeks without surprising me. I watched my driveway for black suburbans, worrying about political fallout as the incident worked its way through the ranks of the state police and news of it possibly even reached the ATF, bureaucrats pointing fingers at each other as to where the breakdown in the system had occurred, and it wasn't hard to imagine becoming the scapegoat for the government's mistake, perhaps even being led away in handcuffs as a result.

It didn't matter, as far as the law was concerned, that I lacked criminal intent, that I had been misinformed as to whether or not I could legally own a firearm, or that I had received much conflicting advice, none of it accurate. Some had said my firearms disability would expire in a certain number of years, much like a bankruptcy. At different times, I was told this period was five, seven, or ten years. At one particular gun store, I was told the only thing to do was to attempt to purchase a gun and see what happened.

The issue at hand seemed to be the sharing of databases between state and federal agencies, but that hardly made sense either, since I had purchased a rifle in Dallas the last time I lived there, about seven years after my commitment. The flaws in the system of national background checks was currently a hot-button issue politically, and I worried about being made an example, perhaps publicly, of someone who had fallen through those cracks.

I locked all my guns away in my father's house, and since I knew the combination to the safe, I told him we would have to install a new lock on the door leading to that room, so that, technically, I would no longer have access to it—the legal term is "constructive possession." My father was having a number of health problems at the time, including a strangely intermittent type of dementia, and was unable to install a new lock, so I wound up doing it myself, to keep myself out. It all seemed such a ridiculous charade.

In the coming weeks, no convoy of federal agents ever rolled down my driveway. I received an unremarkable letter in the mail from the Virginia State Police stating that my sales numbers had been revoked, and that I should feel free to contact them once the issue was resolved. That was all.

THAT FIRST DAY, EXPELLED from my job, I drove home and stood in the house for a minute, listening to the silence, realizing at once that I couldn't stay there. Allison and Phin were in Richmond, three hours away, spending the weekend with Leann

Johnston, the Maid of Honor in our wedding. I hadn't told Allison about any of this yet and needed time to process it for myself. I changed out of my work uniform and threw a few things in my pack and drove to the trailhead at the base of Cove Mountain. I left my truck and hiked up to Dragon's Tooth under the weight of a burden so much like the ones I had carried there before, but in other ways quite different. Perhaps it was only I who was different.

Two and a half arduous miles later, clambering over stony cataracts, and winding up through the switchbacks, I summited the mountain, gulping in the clean air and listening to the music of the wind in the pines. I climbed up to my spot in the high stone saddle of the tooth and lay sprawled in the sun the rest of the day.

"I was grateful to have the afternoon to sweat and suck in fresh mountain air," I later wrote in my journal, "to sit on that rock at the summit and feel the sun on my face, to worship my God, who owns the cattle on a thousand hills, who is not dismayed by evil tidings." It may sound strange, but I felt an unfamiliar sense of excitement, like a schoolchild whose father surprises him one afternoon by taking him out of class for an adventure, to the envy of all his classmates.

By the time I called Allison that night, I had already set up lunch with Jesse for the next day to talk about working together again. I had a plan in place to transition back into tree work as quickly as possible so as to lose no time in getting our cash flow restarted. No way was I going to sit around applying for jobs and being depressed.

Allison was shocked and frightened, as you might imagine. She was afraid that tree work wouldn't be any different this time than it had been before. It was, of course, one of my own fears, and I was even inclined to agree with her; after all, wasn't the very definition of insanity trying the same thing again and expecting a different result?

I did something then that has proven to be an unexpected strength of our marriage, and one that is, unfortunately, often the last thing sensitive young husbands are advised to do. I rebuked my wife. Gently, and with an exhortation to believe that if God was with us, then this time it would be different. We were like the Israelites, going into battle against the same army that had kicked our butts before, only this time, God would fight for us.

I heard myself saying all that and didn't quite know where it had come from. It wasn't something I had thought about beforehand. I was learning to lead. I was learning to believe that salvation would work retrospectively as surely as resurrection would one day unravel death, that even the years I had lost to foolish mistakes and sinful decisions could be redeemed. I was learning that the very basis of fighting fear and depression is a fundamental belief that *God is for us* the same way he was *for* the Israelites. Everything that was happening had been sovereignly ordained, not just for our good, but *for our best*. God had not called us out of Egypt into the wilderness to destroy us, but to reveal himself by great signs and wonders, to make his name great in the victories that would terrify the nations and be faithfully retold for the next three thousand years: fortified cities crumbling, rocks riven and streams gushing out, seas divided, bread raining from the sky, armies slain by a single furious angel, enemies swallowed up by the earth itself.

I was beginning to believe in deliverance.

I met Jesse for lunch and told him the story of what had happened sixteen years ago in Texas, the very story I had so often avoided and attempted to escape, the unwanted history that I had resented for being my miserable record of failure and sin and madness; only this time a funny thing happened. The old shame I had felt in that story was no longer there. It no longer seemed like an airing of dirty laundry or the parading of skeletons from my closet—pick your cliché. It was only the particular set of circumstances from which Jesus had saved me, the trough I had fed at as the Prodigal Son, the bramble patch I had languished in as the Lost Sheep. And I had no reason to doubt that he would deliver me again, from these new trials—not because I deserved it, but for the very same reason he had delivered me in the first place—because it was in his nature to save.

The next day, I was back on a tree job with Jesse, cutting wood and carrying blocks up on my shoulder the way a pirate would carry a barrel of rum, sweating my face off and realizing how soft I had become working in an air-conditioned retail environment.

And this time it *was* different. Work poured in. I had a paying job to do every day but the days I set aside to watch Phin while Allison cleaned houses. We soon had an emergency fund built up again, for the first time in two years. We were even able to take a family vacation to Myrtle Beach, and when we got back I framed in another room in the garage below the house so Allison and I could have our own bedroom again.

"Things are possible now that were not possible before," I wrote in my journal. "I can face, without shame or helplessness, the little financial problems that have bedeviled us for years."

I FOUND AN ATTORNEY in Tarrant County, Texas that agreed to take my case, though it was not easy, and the more phone calls I made, and the more times I related the story, the stranger it seemed to become and the more it began to seem that there must not be any precedent for such a thing, as though I was some castaway who had shown up, sixteen years after being declared legally dead, and asked for his life back. This sort of thing simply did not happen.

My attorney did some asking around in an attempt to find anyone who had ever done this kind of thing before and might know how it worked and what sort of hoops we needed to jump through. This included a number of clerks, and even the District Attorney himself, who, incidentally, had no idea what needed to be done.

The court may have heard a similar case, but even if it had, the records would have been sealed and therefore my attorney could never discover any precedent. We had no way of knowing if we were asking for something that was done frequently, or always flatly refused. Three months later, my attorneys emailed to tell me they had "finally spoken with someone who even knows what kind of case this is."

We eventually pieced together a theory that the records of my commitment had been sealed in 2001 and never shared with NICS, the National Instant Criminal Background Check System, until 2013, when President Obama issued a series of executive orders in response to the Sandy Hook Elementary School Shooting, some of which pertained to databases used by NICS, as well as the sharing of records between state and federal agencies. All that time, it had simply been up to me to answer the question honestly on Form 4473, "have you ever been committed to a mental institution?" and I had the mistaken impression that I was expected to answer that question in the negative once seven years had elapsed, and the matter became (or so I thought) legally void.

My attorney found an obscure provision for the restoration of firearms rights in Texas Health and Safety Code 574.088, the terms of which, although susceptible to broad interpretation, seemed to indicate a way forward. We would have to file a petition, prepare a proposed order, and then, if those were accepted, attend a hearing at the mental health court in Fort Worth, Texas.

Emails from my attorney at that time tended to contain a lot of conditional statements. *If* the court agreed to hear our petition, and *if* we got a hearing, and *if* the judge's personal and political views were favorable... then, we could "hopefully, have your rights restored."

"A court may not grant relief," Texas law states, "unless it makes and enters in the record the following affirmative findings: (1) the person is no longer likely to act in a manner dangerous to public safety; and (2) removing the person's disability to purchase a firearm is in the public interest."

The burden of proof was clearly on me, which, given the political climate on guns during those years of school shootings, threatened executive actions, lobbying by the NRA, and heated emotions on both sides, seemed unlikely in the extreme. I couldn't help but think of my former psychiatrist, who would not write me any sort of letter of recommendation, would never recommend I attempt to live without stifling and possibly even toxic amounts of anti-depressants and mood stabilizers, and would not even inform me how to go about safely weaning myself from them. Permission to own a *gun*? Who was I kidding?

I paid the retainer and set about writing several paragraph-long answers to questions for the petition, including those pertaining to my mental and criminal history, my "reputation," and the "circumstances that led to imposition of the firearms disability."

My attorney worked with me to edit these and put together a packet of other pertinent documents, including a psychological evaluation by a physician—the very same test, incidentally, which my father had recently undergone—and the records of my hospitalization at Trinity Springs Pavilion, all of which was complicated by the secrecy of the mental health court, which refused my attorney's in-person request for my records and required me to submit a signed formal request by U.S. mail, a process that took no fewer than six weeks.

Thanks to their professionalism and objectivity, my attorneys were able to take the statements I provided and strip away the emotion I could not help but include in dredging up some of the most painful memories of my past. Here, for instance, was one of my original sentences: "Per the court's requirements, I saw a psychiatrist in Virginia and took all prescribed anti-depressants and mood-stabilizers for approximately five years until I realized these medicines were doing me no good whatsoever and that the nature of my problems were not chemical or psychological but only the normal problems of learning to be a responsible adult." My attorney's version: "After his departure, Mr. Duncan was required to continue with psychiatric medications and to visit with a psychiatrist in his home state of Virginia where he had returned. Mr. Duncan completely fulfilled all of his obligations."

Weeks, and sometimes entire months, elapsed between emails from my attorneys. Seemingly at every turn, there were new revelations as to which additional forms we would have to submit, and which amendments to the petition I would have to provide, some of which contained the exact same questions I had already answered, only in a slightly different order or with slightly different wording, and others which required me to list, much like the details of a security clearance application, every job I had ever had and every residence I had ever kept with no gaps whatsoever in the timeline.

I began to fear that there was, in actuality, no way back, but that the court was only giving me busy work in the hopes that I would eventually grow tired of the inconvenience and they would be relieved of the nuisance of figuring out what to do with me. Just as I had felt after filing for worker's compensation, I sensed that this process was the punishment, that the process could never be satisfied, never completed; and much like the other consequences of sin in my life, to put it in the same words my creditors had once used about an unpaid debt: "it never goes away."

EIGHTEEN MONTHS PASSED. I worked to build my business, sometimes like a man that deserved to be called insane. In my sleep, I dreamed about cutting trees, and when I came home at night I often staggered from my truck to the door, lightheaded and sweaty, pockets full of sawdust, my arms a gallery of scars from handling brush. I continued to throw out my back periodically, but found that I could, with a quick call to the doctor for a steroid prescription, usually bounce back in a day or two.

"I have had this sense of being in the wilderness with God this past year," I wrote, "out there with no one to help me but him. Rewarded faith has been the single greatest experience of this season. Every day has truly been a miracle... and when I come home, there is a little boy who runs to me at the top of the steps with arms open wide. Surely the Lord has returned to me the years the locust has eaten."

In July, Allison proposed an odd toast, holding up a bite of blueberry crisp on her spoon one night after we put Phin to bed, saying, "Here's to you not having to share the alcohol for the next nine months." Of all the improbable things to come out of a season of emergency transitions, stress, and uncertainty about the future, another new life had begun among us. Our little family would be growing.

In September, my son turned one and took his first faltering steps while I was working on the estate of a customer who would quickly become the best client I ever had. That October, a sonogram revealed we would be having a girl, the first girl born in my family for nearly five generations. Often, late at night, Allison would be reading in bed with a book propped on her belly and the baby would kick hard enough to move the book. Allison would take my hand and lay it flat against a certain spot, both of us scarcely breathing until I felt something live and tremulous and fluttering, my palm pressed to to my daughter's hand on the other side of that wall of flesh. We decided to name her after the greatest woman I had ever known, my late grandmother, Treva, the same grandmother who had once asked me, exasperated upon hearing of another of my break-ups, "Just what kind of girl are you looking for, anyway?"

The following summer, I had the sort of opportunity that rarely comes to those with deep regrets from their past. I drove to Sweet Donkey coffee shop in Roanoke and sat down with Jason Myers, my best friend from college, who, you may remember, had proven his faithfulness to me in the strangest of ways, by reporting me to the police department of Arlington, Texas on a cold February night in 2001. I had not seen him in nearly seventeen years.

"Old friend," he said, reaching out to shake my hand, and I'm afraid it was truer than ever for both of us. He had been in Washington, D.C. that week on business, and had driven four hours out of his way to see me. We had recently spoken on the phone, but there is a kind of talking that only happens in person, and a kind of healing that only comes with a certain kind of talking. We talked with our faces and our hands, with tears burning in our eyes and our hands faltering at the edges of paper napkins, straightening coffee mugs for no apparent reason, turning our faces suddenly to stare at some object outside the coffee shop, glazed with rain, but never even beginning to see it.

All those years, Jason had carried with him the almost unbearable consequence of a single phone call. He had reported me that night out of concern for my life, and then, instead of the relief of rescue had come the horror of my hospitalization, visiting his drugged and diminished friend, who talked with a slurred voice, looked at him with glazed eyes, and could not—the friend that had taken two quarters of symbolic logic with him in college, challenging his proofs by criteria of relentless elegance—could not think with enough concentration to move paper chessmen on the paper chessboard Jason had made and brought with him to the psychiatric ward.

By the time I was released and taken back to Virginia, it had seemed we shared little more than a ruined business partnership and a disaster of which it was painful even to speak. Partly to protect my pride, and partly to shut out any reminder of that nightmare, I had never really spoken to him again. Not until all the breakers and waves of life had passed over us.

Now, for the first time in seventeen years, I was finally able to look my friend in the eye and thank him for what he had done.

BY THE TIME MY daughter was born, Allison and I no longer had any real expectation that I would return to my job at the gun store. Even if my court case was eventually decided—and it appeared, in all likelihood, that it would drag on, unresolved, into the next year—a second child had brought the growing awareness that we would soon outgrow our six-hundred-square-foot living space, the necessity of paying rent again making it unlikely we would be able to survive once more on my old retail manager's income.

I continued to pursue the restoration of my rights, both because my business was going well enough to afford payments to the law firm, and because I was tired of thinking of myself as an outlaw. You may have guessed, by now, that my actual ability to own a firearm was the least of the things at stake in the court's decision. It was the removal, not simply of a legal disability, but of the burden I had carried for seventeen years, the expungement of a stain from my name and public reputation, my honor, my legacy; in short, it had come to symbolize my redemption. If you know anything of the gospel that has transformed my life—more than that: brought me back from the dead—you will see it everywhere in this story, and particularly in the strange way that it ends.

ON DECEMBER 12, 2017, Allison and I packed our little blue Toyota Yaris for exactly the sort of trip it had been made for—in terms of efficiency, if not size and comfort—a nineteen-and-a half-hour drive through the night, non-stop from Richmond, Virginia to Dallas, Texas. I finally had a court date.

"We are embarking on an adventure," I wrote, "the culmination of eighteen months trying to get my gun rights back." We had to leave from Richmond due to an earlier obligation, a jewelry show Allison had scheduled as part of a new side business as a representative for Noon Day Collection.

We had less than twenty-four hours to arrive at my attorney's office in Richardson, Texas—not far from the office tower where I once sat in a cubicle under fluorescent lights typing reports for the lending industry. Our nine-month-old daughter was the wild card in this expedition, not yet weaned and unable to be left behind with my in-laws, as Phin was. We planned to take turns driving while the other slept, but we had no idea whether Treva would sleep in the car, "or whether one of us will recline the passenger seat, hoping to get a few hours sleep, only to face, all the more closely, a red-faced infant screaming her lungs out, her uvula ringing in the back of her throat like the clapper in an alarm."

We drove all those miles of highway I had once put behind me, down through southwest Virginia, diagonally across Tennessee and Arkansas, and into the DFW Metroplex at dusk the following night, just in time to have a brief sit-down with my attorney, Peter Hall, whom I had never had the pleasure of meeting, but who had been working doggedly on my case those past eighteen months. I liked him immediately. He was tall and well-spoken, with short graying hair, and a Texas affectation I found most welcoming: cowboy boots jutting out from beneath his woolen slacks.

We sat down at a conference table, and Peter brought me up to speed. He had never appeared before the judge we would have the next morning, but he had heard that he was fair and reasonable, and that he preferred a strict degree of formality in his courtroom. What mattered more, of course, were his political views, particularly in light of a shooting that had occurred only two months earlier at a church barely three hours outside of Dallas, where a man whose mental health records had never been communicated to the NICS database had essentially fallen through the cracks—much as I had for many years—only he, of course, had used his weapons to kill innocent people, while I had acted in the public interest and proven that I could be trusted. But would the judge see the obvious contrast or would he see all such individuals as an inherent menace to society? We had no way of knowing.

We talked for about an hour, Allison playing with Treva out in the hall, talking to the other attorneys and getting recommendations for a good Tex-Mex restaurant nearby. Peter prepared me for the sorts of questions the judge would likely ask once I was sworn in and took the witness stand. We began with what I called my "Wheel of Fortune Introduction," stating my name and the most immediate particulars of my life, including how I had lost my job upon the discovery of the firearms disability and had driven all day and night to appear before His Honor to get my gun rights back, lest my adorable two children with the sad Disney eyes should starve due to the failure of their bread winner, etc., etc., and so on, as you can imagine, short of saying, Look, I'm a normal guy; here's my normal family and my normal life to prove it, and obviously all that business seventeen years ago was a horrible mistake.

If the judge so permitted us, we would then review all the evidence: the personal letter from the owner of the gun store confirming my reliability and reputation, the doctor's evaluation (whose hand-written notes stated flatly that I had never had any mental problems whatsoever) my own prepared statements of intent and explanation of what happened in 2001, as well as a detailed sort of curriculum vitae that listed all my jobs and residences.

The judge, Peter explained, may or may not have already reviewed the file. By that point, he may or may not be perturbed to be missing his ten o' clock tee time, frowning at a sheaf of documents he had never seen before. He might also be curious, and ask anything at all, and the direction of Peter's questioning would, of course, depend on the sort of signals and demeanor he sensed coming from the judge.

No problem, I said. You box step and I'll box step. You waltz and I'll waltz.

The only other proviso Peter added was to be discrete about mentioning my obvious ownership of firearms during the years that it had actually constituted, unbeknownst to me, a very serious felony. This was a particularly ticklish point, since my safe handling of firearms was both the greatest argument in favor of my character, and the most incriminating admission I had ever made.

What exactly, Allison and I had wondered those long miles from Virginia, was the worst-case scenario here? Might I, at the

judge's whim, actually be arrested and escorted from the courtroom by the bailiff? Our greatest assurance was not any legal
counsel, but the stubborn belief that God had so far orchestrated
every detail of this case for our good. After all, if it hadn't been
for my working relationship with the Virginia State Police—if I
hadn't been known to them at the time when all this came to
light—if, for instance, I had simply walked into any other gun
store in Virginia at any other time in the previous four years
and filled out the paperwork to buy a gun, there was a very good
chance I might have been arrested and incarcerated. We had
only the assurance of our faith, that the Lord would complete
what he had begun and that just as the heart of a king is like water in his hand, so too, the decision of this judge (whose name,
curiously enough, turned out to be Steve King) would be up to
his sovereign rule entirely. I was no one's victim.

WE ATE DINNER AT Franky's, the Tex-Mex restaurant the attorneys had recommended, ordering carne asada and ribeye tacos
with a side of sausage soup, and a margarita "onde rocks" as our
waiter clarified, and it seemed to charm him that my blonde wife
from back east could barely understand what he was saying. Treva,
for her part, began casting her spell upon the entire staff, and one of
the waitresses couldn't help but tickle her in the ribs every time she
walked by our table, drawing wild giggles.

I told Allison I'd forgotten how friendly Texans were.

After dinner, we drove to the Airbnb we had reserved online, an
apartment in an old house on one of the many side streets that led
into lower Greenville, a bar district I had frequented with one of my
first seminary friends, who had gotten drunk and told me his chief
and secret ambition had always been to become, not a youth pastor,
but, in fact, President of the United States.

Greenville was the street that had wowed me as a single man in my mid-twenties, straight from Appalachia, with its lights and noise and bare legs scissoring up the sidewalks into clubs and choppers roaring down the street and party lights and bands playing on rooftop decks—everything I had made a study of for the qualities I thought I lacked: the styles to which I was oblivious, the overly-done sort of bar-hopping women that I struggled to talk to, my low voice lost in the thundering music, and further up the street were the barbershops where I started getting my hair cut in a more fashionable style, and there, too, were the palisades of stuccoed buildings honeycombed with boutiques whose clothes I could not afford, and everywhere I looked it had then been impressed upon me that some great refashioning of my character was necessary if I should ever be happy, and it was not until that very moment, so many years later, looking upon that same street, cold and quiet, that I realized how much of the world I had seen, and how much of that elusive substance I had found elsewhere, and how unexpectedly happiness had come to me under the press of hard labor and suffering, in the silence between the trees on a mountainside as far removed from the glamor of that night scene as another planet altogether, and to think that the woman with whom I had returned to that city had been, all that while, nowhere among it, and that all I had once dreamed of happiness had turned out to be not a conquest, but a gift.

WE ATE BREAKFAST AT La Madeleine on the edge of SMU's Highland Park campus, where I had once taken creative writing classes, and then we drove south on I-75, sitting in bumper-to-bumper traffic on the interchange ramps before we finally got to I-20 and headed west to Fort Worth. Within the hour, we

parked outside the old pink granite courthouse on East Weath-
erford Street, between the world-famous stockyards and Sun-
dance Square.

We found the entrance with a little difficulty since, for security purposes, all the doors had been locked with the exception of
those under the courthouse steps. We passed through the metal
detector, leaving Treva in the stroller with one of the guards smiling down at her while I replaced the contents of my suit pockets
and Allison zipped up her riding boots.

We followed a long hall until we came to the archways of the
rotunda, gazing up through elliptical balconies encircled with
wrought iron railings and scrollwork, up through the second and
third floors, to the dome perhaps one hundred feet above, where
the State Seal of Texas was set in stained glass against the sky.
It seemed the kind of courthouse where a legal thriller of some
kind should be filmed, and apparently, as we found out later,
the courthouse had once made regular appearances in *Walker,
Texas Ranger*.

We rode the elevator up to the second floor and found a bathroom, where I happened upon Peter Hall on his way to the sinks,
and he began to fill me in on a conversation he had already had
that morning with the court attorney.

Apparently she had asked if he had a copy of the order we
would need for the judge to sign if he ruled in our favor—not
necessarily a guarantee that she knew we would be getting such
a ruling, but certainly a very hopeful sign, Peter said.

Allison and Peter and I made small talk in the hall, finding
out that he had a son and daughter, too, and had switched careers later in life from computer programming to law. We waited there perhaps a half hour, with Treva squawking and flirting
with everyone who happened to walk by, and we decided that it
would be best if Allison and Treva stayed in the hall outside the
double doors leading into the chamber, ready to be ushered in
at a moment's notice if the judge wished to call Allison as a witness, but mostly for the sake of not wanting to overstep the yet
unknown protocol of such a hearing.

Finally, a bailiff appeared to inform us that we were the judge's only hearing of the day and that we could go in as soon as we were ready. I kissed Allison and smiled bravely for her before Peter and I entered through a set of heavy wood doors, the brass handles of which were engraved with the state seal. Panels of frosted glass were inset in the doors, beyond which was an antechamber with another set of doors. These, we found, opened onto what was, by far, the most elegant and classic courtroom I had ever seen. I am not versed in the nomenclature, beyond what I have gleaned from courtroom dramas, but the soaring woodwork and paneling of the bench and witness stand made me feel as though I were in one of the episodes of *Perry Mason* I used to watch as a child. Certainly, seventeen years before, sitting in a psychiatric ward of cinderblock walls and windows crisscrossed with reinforced wire, I would have never imagined that the court order that would cause so much shame and suffering in my life could have been handed down from a place so beautiful.

We walked the aisle between a hundred or so empty seats, through a little swinging gate to the defense's table, where Peter's papers were already laid out beside the slender black stem of a microphone and a polished metal pitcher of water. We were the only occupants of the room until the bailiff came in through a side door and instructed us briefly on proper courtroom etiquette, how we should rise when the judge entered and when he left, and so forth. Peter and I sat behind the table making nervous and hushed small talk for perhaps five long minutes before, at last, the same side door opened and the bailiff called, "All rise!"

Peter and I stood, and I happened to think that the last time I had worn that suit and stood in that posture, with my hands clasped in front of me, I had been waiting for Allison to walk down the aisle at our wedding, and this courtroom, too, was a shrine of sorts, a place where solemn oaths were taken before both God and man.

In my peripheral vision I saw the Honorable Steve King enter the courtroom with little more sound than the rustle of his huge and silken robe. No sooner had he gathered up those robes and taken his seat above us, than I heard him say, "Approach the bench," a remark uttered so casually that Peter, at first, seemed hesitant to believe he had heard correctly. He was obviously afraid to assume as much, so sure were we that this was to be an excruciatingly formal procedure. We glanced at each other and stood, coming out from behind the table while Peter made certain, politely, that the judge did not mean for me to take the witness stand.

Silently and impatiently, he beckoned us to come.

We stood there with our shoulders nearly level with the judge's bench and he instructed me to raise my right hand and swear that everything I was about to testify was the truth, the whole truth, and nothing but the truth, so help me God, to which I replied, "Yes, I do."

The judge looked exactly the way you would expect and even hope for a judge to appear: an intensity and purity to the pale eyes set beneath his white hair. At this point he turned, rather abruptly to Peter and said, "Now, I know who he is, but who are you?"

Peter apologized and introduced himself, after which the judge seemed satisfied that he had sufficiently set the man back on his heels. "You may proceed," he said.

Keeping to our script, Peter turned and asked me to introduce myself and tell a little bit about my particulars, which I did, getting as far as where I had worked at the time of the discovery of my firearms disability, at which point the judge interrupted and said, "Let's cut right to the chase."

When Peter offered him a copy of our exhibits he only said, "This is a paperless court. I've read the entire file and I'm very familiar with it. My understanding is," he said, leveling his gaze at me, "you came down to Texas and started a business, you got overstressed, you had this breakdown, you got treatment, it *worked*, and you haven't had a reoccurrence."

At each of these phrases I nodded, ready to say, "Yes, Your Honor," but not sure he was quite done, and only at this last phrase managing to get it out, but he was already continuing as he reached for a fat black fountain pen lying at his elbow, a Waterford or a Mont Blanc from the looks of it.

"I've decided that we are going to grant it," he said, motioning for a copy of the order and unscrewing the cap from his pen. "You know, we're the only county doing these," he remarked, almost casually, to Peter.

Stunned, I watched the judge sign his name in thick blue ink, what I would have told you, right there, under oath, was the most beautiful autograph I have ever seen. Just like that, with an official flourish of his pen, he granted the very thing I had longed for those seventeen years. Just like that, it was as though the nightmare had never happened.

The providence of that moment was rendered even more incredible by the conversation I now overheard between the judge and my attorney. He told Peter that he was a member of a legal association related to firearms rights and had recently urged the association to begin doing more for the cause of rights restoration. I realized then that not only was the Honorable Judge Steve King *not* an anti-gun activist, he was actually an *advocate* for firearms rights.

If, all those years before, my nervous breakdown had occurred anywhere else in the great state of Texas but Tarrant County, I would, in all likelihood, have never gotten my rights back. If I had appeared before any other judge—I was beginning to sense that the way had been prepared before me. There had been no occasion to plead my case. No calling of witnesses, no dissembling on the part of the judge. Before I had even arrived, the decision had been made.

Allison was taken aback by how quickly Peter and I reappeared from the chamber, the slack look on her face indicating she wasn't at all sure what it might mean, and when I smiled and said, "We got it," and took her in my arms, she began to cry. Even some time later, standing outside the courthouse blinking in the sun at the bright white photocopy of the order, I couldn't help but stare at the word GRANTED in disbelief, even taking a picture of it with my phone, as though the paper copies in triplicate I held were not proof enough, not substantially corporeal that they might not vanish in an instant as though they were only parcel to some wonderful but fleeting dream.

We enlisted the aid of a man passing through the square to take a picture of the three of us, standing there on the granite steps of the courthouse, all of us smiling, my arm around Allison, and Treva in Allison's arms and the orders folded and tucked in my suit pocket, and the unalterable words of the judge they bore were these:

"IT IS THEREFORE ORDERED, ADJUDGED, AND DECREED: The application of Ian Jon Duncan for relief pursuant to Texas Health & Safety Code 574.088 is hereby GRANTED;

Ian Jon Duncan does not suffer from a mental disability;

Ian Jon Duncan does not pose a danger to himself or the public;

Removal of Ian Jon Duncan's disability is in the public interest;

Ian Jon Duncan's disability is hereby set aside."

EPILOGUE

IT IS A HOT, dry day on the summit at Dragon's Tooth, and no pools of rainwater in the pitted surface of the boulders, only heat waves dancing over the stones, heat that lifts a buzzard, circling, in an updraft of warmth. A breeze drives the blackflies from the rock in mad, buzzing arcs; a breeze borne across mountaintops receding into the blue distance, ridge upon ridge. Many of those ranges are dark as an approaching storm; others are the color of the ocean, still others like a slate flagstone, and some are the same watercolor tint as the sky, separated only by the uncertain atmosphere that lies along the horizon.

Standing on the tooth, I can barely discern the pyramid shape of Peaks of Otter, forty miles away to the north, covered in the haze of a long dry-spell, a milky fog like looking through linen held close to my eye.

The breeze is moving the branches of the pines, and the closest brush their needles across the rock like fingernails on a lover's back. The rocks are the color of an elephant, their surface pocked and scarred and uneven like hide stretched taut over bones. Fine grit turns between my boot soles and the rocks when I clamber over them. Beneath me, the rock is the most solid, unmovable place in the entire world. Underfoot there is no subtle give as there is on the ground, as layer upon layer of old leaves compress; here there is not even the gentle sponge of house floors granting tiny concessions between wood fibers.

Higher still, I bend to grip the rock with my hands, climbing the final pitch as the rock narrows, where, if I allowed myself to look, the distance to the ground might become dizzying. I am focused on the rock, but I do not have to think; my boots find the same places they always have, a rough spot here, good for gripping, there a projection where the arch of my sole fits just so. I can feel the hard quartz ridges under my hands and I see them, weathered white like knuckles shining through skin. Between the ridges are sandy, small-of-back hollows where lichens decorate the stone in flaky blooms.

I'm on the very top now, barely wide enough for hands and knees, and I turn carefully and sit in the seat sculpted, it seems, just for me: a dimple between the elephant's shoulders. I unlace my boots and peel off my socks and hang my feet over the edge, spreading my toes while the breeze blows through them. I look down into the valley and see how laughably small the world is, how ridiculous the little metallic ant of a sports car winding along the asphalt ribbon below. I can hold my fingers a quarter inch apart and fit them over houses and barns and silos. Despite all human ambition, the city I came from is no more than a discoloration in the valley, a glacier of roads and housing caught between the hills for a few centuries while the mountain watches.

Closer by there are fields, green in swaths where the tractor passed towards me, and silver where it moved away. Hay bales dot the mown expanse like random monuments, while the grass of an uncut field rolls in the wind like a blanket held and shaken. Trees along the fence line cast perfect shadows beside them. A cloud floats across the sun, taking the light, and then it floods back, and it is the tree and the whole bright landscape that reappears—the shadow seems to have remained all along.

I don't remember how long I've been here, and I haven't seen enough yet to leave. I stare at the rambling blue mountains until I am sure I will still see them when I close my eyes a thousand miles away; sure that I will feel the sun-soaked rock under my hands and hear the wind, pure and clean, blowing through the branches—a holy sound like air through a cathedral spire, like breath through a flute without notes—and I know I will come to this place often, even when the only mountains around me are the geometric outlines of skyscrapers, and my only view the heat baking off flat, pale concrete.

This is the mountain where God met me, where he interrupted my life, where he struck me, where he healed me, where he directed storms and hung rainbows and measured my steps along the trail, planning to perfection the very second he would bring my wife out from behind a shaking rhododendron, as surely as he presented Eve to Adam.

This is the mountain where I worked out my salvation with fear and trembling. This is my nest in the wilderness, this hill my ebenezer. As long as I last, as long as my heart and my limbs hold out in climbing here, I will come.

ABOUT THE AUTHOR

IAN DUNCAN is the author of a trilogy of bio-thrillers, including *Cordyceps, Cordyceps Resurgentis,* and *Cordyceps Victoriosis.* He is an MFA candidate in the creative writing program at New Saint Andrews College, cohost of the literary podcast *The Notion Club,* and is currently at work on the forthcoming adventure novel, *Mouribon Cave.* He met his wife, Allison, on the Appalachian Trail, and is now the proud father of Phinehas, Treva, and Ransom. He still frequents that strange collection of rocks on the summit of Cove Mountain called Dragon's Tooth. Discover more at IanDuncanBooks.com.